HOW TO BE A SUCCESSF

SUE DYSON was brought up
qualified as a translator before b
graduate in French and English,
and Executive Secretary's Diploma exams with the
highest marks ever awarded. She has taught secretarial
students as a part-time lecturer at Scarborough Technical College. Now a full-time writer, she nevertheless
keeps her hand in temping and translating. She was
LCCI/Sony UK 'Secretary of the Year' in 1987.

STEPHEN HOARE was born and brought up in South
London. After three years as an English teacher, he
worked as an editor in educational publishing before
becoming a lecturer in publishing at the London College
of Printing. He is now Features Editor with a major
trade newspaper.

Overcoming Common Problems Series

The ABC of Eating
Coping with anorexia, bulimia and
compulsive eating
JOY MELVILLE

Beating the Blues
SUSAN TANNER AND JILLIAN
BALL

Beating Job Burnout
DR DONALD SCOTT

Being the Boss
STEPHEN FITZSIMON

Birth Over Thirty
SHEILA KITZINGER

Body Language
How to read others' thoughts by their
gestures
ALLAN PEASE

Bodypower
DR VERNON COLEMAN

Calm Down
How to cope with frustration and anger
DR PAUL HAUCK

Comfort for Depression
JANET HORWOOD

Common Childhood Illnesses
DR PATRICIA GILBERT

Complete Public Speaker
GYLES BRANDRETH

Coping with Anxiety and Depression
SHIRLEY TRICKETT

Coping with Depression and Elation
DR PATRICK McKEON

Coping with Stress
DR GEORGIA WITKIN-LANOIL

Coping with Suicide
DR DONALD SCOTT

Coping with Thrush
CAROLINE CLAYTON

**Coping Successfully with Your Child's
Asthma**
DR PAUL CARSON

**Coping Successfully with Your Child's Skin
Problems**
DR PAUL CARSON

**Coping Successfully with Your Hyperactive
Child**
DR PAUL CARSON

Coping Successfully with Your Irritable Bowel
ROSEMARY NICOL

Curing Arthritis Diet Book
MARGARET HILLS

Curing Arthritis – The Drug-free Way
MARGARET HILLS

**Curing Coughs, Colds and Flu – the
Drug-free Way**
MARGARET HILLS

Curing Illness – The Drug-free Way
MARGARET HILLS

Depression
DR PAUL HAUCK

Divorce and Separation
ANGELA WILLANS

The Dr Moerman Cancer Diet
RUTH JOCHEMS

The Epilepsy Handbook
SHELAGH McGOVERN

**Everything You Need to Know about
Adoption**
MAGGIE JONES

**Everything You Need to Know about
Contact Lenses**
DR ROBERT YOUNGSON

**Everything You Need to Know about Your
Eyes**
DR ROBERT YOUNGSON

**Everything You Need to Know about the
Pill**
WENDY COOPER AND TOM SMITH

Everything You Need to Know about Shingles
DR ROBERT YOUNGSON

Family First Aid and Emergency Handbook
DR ANDREW STANWAY

Overcoming Common Problems Series

Feverfew
A traditional herbal remedy for migraine
and arthritis
DR STEWART JOHNSON

Fight Your Phobia and Win
DAVID LEWIS

Getting Along with People
DIANNE DOUBTFIRE

Goodbye Backache
DR DAVID IMRIE WITH COLLEEN
DIMSON

Helping Children Cope with Divorce
ROSEMARY WELLS

Helping Children Cope with Grief
ROSEMARY WELLS

How to be a Successful Secretary
SUE DYSON AND STEPHEN HOARE

How to Be Your Own Best Friend
DR PAUL HAUCK

How to Control your Drinking
DRS W. MILLER AND R. MUNOZ

How to Cope with Stress
DR PETER TYRER

How to Cope with your Child's Allergies
DR PAUL CARSON

**How to Cope with Tinnitus and Hearing
Loss**
DR ROBERT YOUNGSON

How to Cure Your Ulcer
ANNE CHARLISH AND DR BRIAN
GAZZARD

How to Do What You Want to Do
DR PAUL HAUCK

How to Enjoy Your Old Age
DR B. F. SKINNER AND M. E.
VAUGHAN

How to Improve Your Confidence
DR KENNETH HAMBLY

How to Interview and Be Interviewed
MICHELE BROWN AND GYLES
BRANDRETH

How to Love a Difficult Man
NANCY GOOD

How to Love and be Loved
DR PAUL HAUCK

How to Make Successful Decisions
ALISON HARDINGHAM

How to Move House Successfully
ANNE CHARLISH

How to Pass Your Driving Test
DONALD RIDLAND

How to Say No to Alcohol
KEITH McNEILL

How to Spot Your Child's Potential
CECILE DROUIN AND ALAIN DUBOS

How to Stand up for Yourself
DR PAUL HAUCK

**How to Start a Conversation and Make
Friends**
DON GABOR

How to Stop Feeling Guilty
DR VERNON COLEMAN

How to Stop Smoking
GEORGE TARGET

How to Stop Taking Tranquillisers
DR PETER TYRER

Hysterectomy
SUZIE HAYMAN

If Your Child is Diabetic
JOANNE ELLIOTT

Jealousy
DR PAUL HAUCK

Learning to Live with Multiple Sclerosis
DR ROBERT POVEY, ROBIN DOWIE
AND GILLIAN PRETT

Living Alone – A Woman's Guide
LIZ McNEILL TAYLOR

Living with Grief
DR TONY LAKE

Overcoming Common Problems Series

Overcoming Common Problems

HOW TO BE
A SUCCESSFUL SECRETARY

Sue Dyson and Stephen Hoare

SHELDON PRESS
LONDON

First published in Great Britain in 1990 by
Sheldon Press, SPCK, Marylebone Road, London NW1 4DU

British Library Cataloguing in Publication Data
Dyson, Sue
   How to be a successful secretary.
   1. Secretaryship
   I. Title   II. Hoare, Stephen   III. Series
   651.3'741

   ISBN 0-85969-598-0

Typeset by Deltatype Ltd, Ellesmere Port, Cheshire
Printed in Great Britain by Biddles Ltd, Guildford and Kings Lynn

Contents

Acknowledgements

The authors would like to thank the following people for their assistance in the preparation of this book: Carole Vivier (without whom the project would not have got off the ground!); June Tatum (Executive Secretaries' Club); Margaret Evans (Senior Examinations Officer, Secretarial Studies, at the London Chamber of Commerce and Industry) (LCCI); Wendy Syer (PA to Sir Campbell Adamson); Isabella Szredzki (PR Officer, Alfred Marks Bureau); Juliet Hepburn (Industrial Society); Mr and Mrs Richard Adams; Liz Aydon; Lynda McDonnell; Lola Hatmil; Ruth Cocksedge; Brian Spence (Alexis Personnel); Sir Terence Conran; Annalisa Hamilton; Marjorie Hoare; Susan Beck; Helen Hutty (Group Finance Director, Cecil MacDonald & Co Ltd); Alison Bailey; Rory Henneker; RSA Examinations Board; AMSPAR (Association of Medical Secretaries, Practice Administrators and Receptionists); IAS (Institute of Agricultural Secretaries); ALS (Association of Legal Secretaries); IPQS (Institute of Qualified Private Secretaries); APAS (Association of Personal Assistants and Secretaries); EAPS (European Association of Professional Secretaries); APEX/GMU (Association of Professional, Executive, Clerical and Computer Staff/General, Municipal, Boilermakers and Allied Trades Union); Principals, Departmental Staff and Students of: Newcastle Polytechnic, Lucie Clayton Secretarial College, Scarborough Technical College, St Godric's College, Merton College, Pitman College and Humberside Business School.

NOTE:
There are quite a few male secretaries around these days. It's our earnest hope that the 1990s will see an end to all the eyebrow-raising and innuendo, and leave gifted individuals of both sexes free to consider secretarial work as a first-choice career.

Nevertheless, whilst the ratio of female secretaries to male remains around 99:1, it's not surprising that the language of secretarial work tends to portray secretaries as if they were all women. We have tried to avoid this inherent sexism wherever possible, but if we have occasionally fallen into the trap, we do

ACKNOWLEDGEMENTS

apologize. Please assume that 'he' and 'she' are interchangeable; there are no hidden implications, and we have no desire to offend any secretary – male or female.

Introduction

This book deals with the concept of the successful secretary.

There are still plenty of people (some of them secretaries) who believe that it isn't possible to be a secretary *and* be successful. In other words, the very fact of entering secretarial work is an admission of a failure to do anything more demanding or worthwhile. To paraphrase the old adage: 'those who can, do: those who can't, become secretaries.'

Today's competent secretary, particularly in London, can expect to be courted with offers of high salaries and bonuses, excellent working conditions and fringe benefits such as dress allowances and free meals. Nevertheless, money alone does not automatically confer status upon an employee.

No matter how high she aims and how lofty the position she attains, the secretary remains a perpetual 'number two' in any organizational structure. No matter how talented she may be, a secretary's worth will always tend to be judged in terms of her boss's success, rather than on the merits of projects which she has executed on her own.

A recent job advertisement placed by a Baker Street firm announced that their 'Sherlock Holmes' was looking for a 'Watson'. Unfortunately, the popular image of Watson is of a bumbling incompetent, perhaps slightly redeemed by his unshakeable loyalty and proficiency with a service revolver – a comparison which is not at all flattering to today's high-flying PA. Just as years of low-budget films have created a caricature out of Conan Doyle's original conception, so popular myths and misconceptions continue to distort the picture of polished professionalism which career secretaries seek to project.

Not everyone wants to be 'number one', of course; but most of us require recognition for our efforts, and room to achieve success within the limits of our own job, talents and expectations.

For the first time, concerted attempts are being made to change the popular image of the secretary. It's now reasonable to suggest that secretarial work can be a career in its own right, with its own opportunities for personal pride and achievement; and for the top

1

secretary, it has also become a fast-moving world of expensive lunches, travel, VIPs and money, money, money . . .

At the other end of the scale, a secretary can also be a downtrodden single parent slaving away at a manual typewriter in Grimsby for £5,000 per year – and *no* fringe benefits beyond the odd glass of sherry at Christmas.

Small wonder then that the question of exactly what a secretary is, does and ought to be capable of doing continues to excite public interest. Is she a sexy young thing in flimsy crêpe blouses, or an old battleaxe encased in navy blue crimplene suits? An executive high-flier with carphone, Filofax and a degree in Economics, or a YTS clerical trainee with GCSE Keyboarding Skills and a tenuous grasp of the English language? Administrator or machine operator? Surrogate wife? Her boss's fellow-professional – or simply the office slave? Despite a never-ending and very lively debate, no-one has yet come up with a satisfactory definition of the secretary, since the secretary is all things to all jobs.

The National Council for Vocational Qualifications seeks to put a stop to all this. By defining the precise level at which office work becomes secretarial work, and indicating where an office junior steps onto the first rung of the secretarial career ladder, NCVQ is going to put quite a few cats among the pigeons.

There's no doubt that the vast majority of professional secretaries welcome any attempt to enhance the status of secretaries and dispel popular prejudices about their work. Yet as the job itself becomes more complex and demanding – and indeed unattainable for those of limited ability – how many people will want to train to be professional secretaries for a new generation and a new century?

Will it really be worth all the effort, just to be 'number two'?

1
Part of the Management Team?

According to line management theory, everyone within an organization is graded according to job function and seniority. But in a typical company organization chart the secretary may well be out on a limb. She has a purely 'staff' relationship with her boss, that is to say, she is responsible to him alone for everything she does. Although her actions are restricted by having to report to her boss, she does not (on the whole) have the compensation of knowing that someone else is below her in the organizational structure who has to answer to her.

Secretaries may be accustomed to operate within a senior management environment and even represent their boss at Board level: yet they don't enjoy the career structure and prospects which any manager would expect. What the secretary does have is a 'special', very personal, working relationship with her boss which can generate resentment, as well as respect, among other bosses and even junior managers.

A special relationship

The 'special' relationship between boss and secretary does not come automatically with the job. Nevertheless, without that relationship no working partnership – and no secretary – can be really successful. Over a period of time, the secretary comes to know her boss better than anyone else in the organization, and possibly as well as any member of his own family. As a result, the boss often shares confidential information with her, and entrusts her with emotional burdens which may have little to do with office life.

The closeness of such a relationship can have drawbacks for the secretary whose sense of loyalty may conflict with her own ambitions to progress within the organization. Understandably, few bosses would be keen to lose a good secretary and *confidante* – particularly to a rival manager who might make good use of any personal information which he could extract from her. Since most senior secretaries have a fierce sense of professionalism, this may seem an unlikely scenario. But for some bosses, it's a very real fear.

3

Private life and working life are inextricably linked for the senior manager, and many secretaries have found their duties extended not just to coffee-making but to choosing family presents, doing shopping, booking theatre tickets and planning social engagements. One secretary we spoke to complained that the boss's wife used to come to the office in the morning and dump her dirty washing in the secretary's 'in' basket for her to take to the laundry or dry cleaner's!

It is, of course, a valid argument that the secretary should take over some of the boss's chores because her time costs the firm less. For a manager to make a cup of tea might cost the firm £5; for a secretary, the same amount of time might cost only 20p. The secretary whose duties extend beyond the narrow confines of her job description is, in theory, freeing her boss to do what he is paid for.

The other side of the argument is that the secretary is a skilled professional in her own right, not a housekeeper and all-purpose dogsbody. Surely her time is also valuable, and although helping her boss to make essential social arrangements might be a good use of time, darning her boss's socks isn't the best use of her skills!

Most secretaries accept that they will have to devote a small proportion of their time to 'non-secretarial' duties. Some enjoy doing so and regard such responsibilities as a mark of trust. Even a top-flight secretary may be expected to perform relatively menial tasks (such as making the tea) – it all depends upon the boss's personality and management style. However, the secretary is not an 'office wife', as the media so often like to suggest, and clearly this view of the relationship is set to change as more women become managers. Also, the gradual influx of male secretaries looks like bringing about a subtle change in attitudes. Would you – a male boss – ask your male secretary to darn your socks?

Anyone in a position of responsibility both gives and receives orders or instructions. Yet despite the responsibilities inherent in their jobs, many people believe that secretaries exist only to take orders. There's still the sexist myth that secretaries are well-paid tea-makers, that they are chosen merely to enhance the image of a male boss. Some secretaries even behave in a servile way, because they believe this is expected of them.

As long as you are a secretary you will always be 'number two'. Many secretaries have given this as their reason for leaving secretarial work, and it's also thought to be one reason for the shortage of new recruits to secretarial college. However, while the job of secretary is undeniably a support role, the professional secretary ought never to be seen as servile.

Teamwork

A secretary can gain or lose responsibility according to the boss's level of trust, experience and management style. No secretarial job is inherently rewarding: it's rather like a lucky dip. Your working life and job satisfaction will always tend to be in someone else's hands. To quote Isabella Szredzki, PR Officer for Alfred Marks, 'It's a . . . dilemma, because the secretary is the boss's immediate junior, or the one that's closest to him. But in terms of responsibility, she has less in her own right than other managers, because she is given tasks that wouldn't be given to managers.'

Are some bosses more trusting and more willing to delegate? Certainly. Just as there are good and bad secretaries, so there are good and bad bosses. To be a good boss implies an ability to manage the scarce resources of time, money, information and staff. A boss who busies himself with trivia is wasting his time; a boss who can't delegate is wasting the resources of his staff.

There's an apocryphal story about a boss who was so determined to be in control of his office that he opened, read and replied to every item of incoming mail, no matter how trivial. He was so obsessive and distrustful that when he went away on holiday to Southend he made his secretary travel down from London each day to bring him the mail.

He's an extreme type, but he's not alone! Here are some other types which you may recognize:

- *the offloader*: he gets rid of all the boring or difficult jobs which he doesn't want to do himself by giving them to his secretary and calling it delegation. She gets all the blame if things go wrong, but if there's any credit going, it's all his;
- *the one-man-band*: determined to do absolutely everything himself, even if it kills him, because (as every schoolboy knows) if you want a job doing properly, you have to do it yourself. Won't even give his secretary the authority to order a box of paperclips without looking over her shoulder as she fills in the requisition;

- *the Lord High Executioner*: glares at the world from behind his mahogany desk and makes it his policy to shout at everyone at least once a day. Enjoys sacking people, so disagree with him at your peril. Is invariably right. If any project proves successful it was entirely his idea;

- *the ignoramus*: joined the firm as tea boy in 1938 and worked his way up from the shop floor. Tells everyone he is a self-made man and got all his education at the University of Life. Likes to use long words but doesn't know what they mean. Thinks he can spell;

- *the playboy* (otherwise known as *Sid the Sexist*): a confirmed male chauvinist pig. The only figure work he's interested in is yours! His conversation is peppered with innuendoes but he'd probably run a mile if you took him up on any of his offers. Probably married and going bald;

- *the wimp*: a Peter Pan figure who will never grow into his job, because it will always be far too big for him. Usually found sheltering behind Wendy – a fiercely competent secretary who would die rather than reveal his shortcomings;

- *the socialite*: cannot bear to be alone in his office working quietly. Always out at lunch, 'on-site', convening an *ad hoc* meeting or simply 'co-ordinating' (i.e. wandering round the building with a memo in his hand);

- *the Amazon*: a holy terror in designer trousers. This exclusively female executive is particularly prevalent in fashion houses, advertising and journalism. Has got to the top by drinking her male colleagues under the table. Smokes at least 100 cigarettes a day (three at once). A veritable slave driver, with no sympathy for human frailty;

- *the organizer*: organizes everything and everybody. Spends several hours each day with his collection of Filofaxes (one is not enough) writing lists of things he won't have time to do and people he won't have time to meet, or playing with his database. Appears to do a great deal but in fact accomplishes nothing.

Recognition and status

It's still largely true to say that a secretary's status is derived from that of her boss. Under new provisions heralded by the National Council for Vocational Qualifications the secretary will be recognized as a professional in her own right: an employee with a certain level of qualification and, presumably, certain levels of salary and status to match.

But that's all in the future. As things stand the secretary's fortunes must be linked to those of her boss at every turn. Status depends on the boss's promotion, and so secretary and boss are in a very real sense a team, making a collective effort for mutual benefit. Salary (in the private sector) will depend upon recognition of excellence, and that recognition can only come from the boss. A bad relationship with a boss, or working for a manager who lacks prospects or ambition, can seriously hamper a secretary's career. And of course if a manager will not delegate, there's no opportunity for a secretary to prove her worth.

The refusal to delegate may not stem from a personality problem on the part of the boss; it may result from a lack of trust. Every ounce of trust has to be earned by a secretary and it can take months to build up the sort of good working relationship in which tasks can be freely shared or delegated. Wendy Syer (PA to Sir Campbell Adamson, Chairman of the Abbey National Building Society), comments, 'It probably took us three to six months to get to know each other really well. It gets better all the time!'

There can be a great sense of pride and achievement in creating the perfect 'symbiotic' boss/secretary relationship. On the other hand, this kind of situation can all too easily tempt a secretary to 'empire-build': to create a private kingdom which only she (and perhaps her boss) can enter or understand. Protecting the relationship in this way is bad for the organization. The secretary can become indispensable and communications can break down if she's the only agent of information transfer between the boss and the rest of the organization. What happens on the day she breaks her leg and is off work for three months? As Wendy Syer says, 'It's no good a secretary being indispensable. Someone should be able to walk into this office and be able to look after the boss from day one.'

The secretary's management skills

All too often a secretary's management skills are not seen as managing at all. The idea of the secretary as manager is still a long way from gaining universal acceptance.

Since senior secretaries and PAs work so closely with the highest levels of management, it should be reasonable to suppose that they would be viewed as a useful pool of skilled labour from which to select management personnel. Not so. The secretary who does become a manager is still a rarity and tends to achieve management status in spite of her secretarial background, rather than because of it.

Although today's secretaries exercise management skills every day just to carry out their jobs competently, the supportive secretarial role remains largely alien to the concept of the independently-functioning manager, who is expected to display enterprise, initiative and authority.

Anyone who has been a senior secretary will know that secretaries have to display all these qualities on a daily basis. Secretaries are great problem-solvers and troubleshooters and excellent managers of time, information and people. Who creates all the office systems? Who saves the day when the conference venue is double-booked and there's only twenty-four hours to go? Who calms irate telephone callers and persuades people to do things they don't want to do . . . and all the time never stops smiling? The secretary.

Perhaps in an attempt to improve both the status of senior secretaries and their potential for promotion to management, some organizations have moved towards the concept of the 'management assistant'. There's no difference in terms of duties between a management assistant, a personal assistant and a senior secretary, but there's little doubt which title carries the most kudos. It's also the most truly descriptive of what a senior secretary does. To quote Juliet Hepburn, Head of the Secretarial Development Department of the Industrial Society:

We can identify what we believe secretaries to be, and our definition of a secretary is that the secretary assists management to do the job. Now, that will imply that at a certain level secretaries can be called management assistants, because that's what they should be doing. That would not apply all the way down the line, because there should – as with any management strata – be some sort of delineated progression: but nobody has yet managed to identify what that is.

So where does the manager's job stop and the secretary's start?

To a large extent it depends on individual needs, talents and preferences. It would be foolish for a manager to thrust high-level figure-work onto his secretary just for the sake of delegation, knowing full well that she hates figure-work, has no numerical ability and is bound to make dozens of mistakes. That's off-loading, not delegation, and it's ultimately counterproductive.

On the other hand, if the secretary is willing and able to take on a complex task, then there is a strong case for delegation. The manager's workload will be eased and the secretary will be motivated by the opportunity to show what she can do. Juliet Hepburn comments:

> One would expect a senior secretary to be competent in accepting and dealing with delegated work at a particular level. Where a secretary is competent, able and qualified to deal with a particular project of his or her manager . . . what you are relying on is not the competence and the ability of the secretary to take it on but the ability of the manager to delegate that task. And the competence of the secretary therefore would depend upon the competence of the manager.

Job satisfaction

Job satisfaction is a relatively new concept, particularly for secretaries. The economic constraints of recent years have made getting and keeping a job – any job – the most important consideration. Now, with the easing of the economic climate, highly-skilled workers in any trade or profession can begin to be more selective and demanding in their choice of employer.

Being a secretary still means all things to all people. Job titles and gradings vary just as much as the jobs themselves and the pay and conditions attached to them. The shortage of secretarial staff has meant a huge rise in salaries in the South-East, and opportunities for young and inexperienced staff to get into top jobs paying top money. Unfortunately, this hasn't done much to improve the morale of the middle-aged secretary with years of experience and excellent qualifications, who finds herself on the same grade and salary scale as a girl half her age, who appears to have neither qualifications nor experience. There's still no clear career progression for secretaries, and most don't have the chance to increase their job satisfaction by being promoted on merit.

Everyone needs job satisfaction. As A. H. Maslow observed, once people have the basic requirements of food, shelter and warmth, what they are really looking for in a job is much more intangible. When you have enough money to pay for all the consumer goods and services you want, the offer of still more money becomes progressively less important. Self-esteem and fulfilment are far more important than pay rises to most people who earn good salaries – and, of course, these needs are far harder to satisfy.

The really effective incentives – the ones which actually make people more productive – are not automatically present in secretarial work; some of them have to be earned, negotiated, even fought for. A manageable level of responsibility, freedom to organize one's own workload, flexibility, variety, respect, praise and the opportunity for personal development and achievement – all these are important but by no means automatic. Many of them depend upon the attitude of the individual boss, a feature which is more pronounced in secretarial work than in most other jobs.

How can secretaries achieve real job satisfaction? If we talk in terms of personal responsibility and authority, few secretaries are given the chance to make top-level decisions, even though they may have researched much of the information on which a decision was based. This is bad news if you want to be in the limelight, but it can be very satisfying just to know that you have contributed towards an important corporate decision.

Unlike the struggling junior manager, the senior secretary also has the satisfaction of spending every working day in a prestigious and powerful environment. Depending on the type of job she has, she may also have the opportunity to travel the world and meet important people. Secretaries certainly can move in worlds which wouldn't be open to them as members of other professions. Given talent and the knack of being in the right place at the right time, some secretaries may also become members of such milieux in their own right. But it's well worth remembering that secretarial work is no longer an automatic 'back door' to other careers (if indeed it ever was). If you want to be an astronaut there are better ways of going about it than becoming a secretary at NASA.

Just how satisfying is it to be surrounded by the trappings of power if you aren't wielding any power yourself? Status by association is enough for some people. It's a privilege to be at the top, working at the heart of high-level decision-making, and yet not find your head on the block every time a mistake is made.

But the world is changing rapidly. The vast majority of careers have opened their doors to women and women are seen to succeed in the public eye. No matter how much she is disliked in some quarters, it's a fact that Margaret Thatcher has been an inspiration to a whole generation of women, forcing them to take stock of their own achievements and career potential. It's rather unfashionable now to derive satisfaction from a seemingly low-status, unregarded job. Some women feel driven by the pressure which has always existed for men: the need to achieve status and recognition and to be rewarded for results, hard work and enterprise. Women now have accepted the challenge, and compete on equal terms with men.

With hard work and enterprise comes stress. Many people have discovered quite late on in their careers that one of the great compensations of a secretarial career is its relative lack of stress. As Wendy Syer comments, 'There's a thin line between having a *demanding* job and a *stressful* one.' It may be a narrow difference but it's a real one. Secretaries don't always have to take full responsibility for their actions; they're out of the public eye and they generally enjoy a secure working relationship. The reverse of this is the fact that secretaries also don't always get the recognition they deserve. It really hurts when your boss takes the credit for something which you carried through on your own, perhaps with very little encouragement.

Developing your skills

Job satisfaction has a lot to do with knowing what you want from your job and from your boss and from understanding your own capabilities. Managers and their secretaries have to work together as a team, and that means making the most of talents on both sides, whilst also co-operating to minimize each other's weaknesses.

Much has been made of training secretaries to service management. But what about training managers to use secretaries? Juliet Hepburn of the Industrial Society is only too aware of the problem. Most first-time bosses haven't a clue about what secretaries can do and often fail to recognize their potential to carry out complex delegated work. For this reason the Industrial Society now runs courses designed to help bosses and their secretaries to get the best from each other.

But it's still largely up to individual secretaries and bosses to work out a satisfactory arrangement which allows each of them to do what they do best. In many instances this means the secretary has to train her boss! Whether overt or subtle, the influence of a secretary over her boss can be quite considerable.

On the other hand, the power of the boss to make or break a secretary's career is also a force to be reckoned with. No boss is going to be very keen to see a good secretary go, so it's in his interest to keep her exactly where she is. On the other hand, many bosses would say that a secretary whose single preoccupation is her own career progression into management probably isn't much use to them. She will tend not to accept routine tasks, will question every decision and will be concerned with her own ambitions rather than the good of the organization. These bosses would be unlikely to block their secretaries' career ambitions but would be equally unlikely to encourage them.

Some bosses are, of course, rather more altruistic and far-sighted, and any ambitious secretary who is able to make an ally of her boss is fortunate indeed. Nevertheless, we are left with the unanswered question: Is the ideal secretary really one who is not personally ambitious?

A round peg in a round hole

What personal qualities make for a happy and successful secretary? Juliet Hepburn told us:

> I have said publicly that I think women have some qualities that are admirably suited to being secretaries – I really do. I believe that they have intuitive communication skills, which are exhibited in lots of ways. I mean, for instance, that there aren't so many men . . . who know instinctively if a baby is crying for no reason at all, or whether it's got a dirty nappy. (Women) are extremely good in their private lives at planning. Take the example of Christmas dinner. You know, with two aged aunts who are pretty doddery and two sets of parents who aren't talking to each other, and getting it all organized.

12

This is the popular view of the secretary as self-effacing, capable, intuitive . . . and almost always female. Is this sexist rubbish or is there a grain of truth in it? Is it all a question of sex, personality or upbringing – or a combination of all three?

Is it really necessary to be a subservient person in order to be a happy secretary? Top secretaries and PAs would argue emphatically not! Whilst she may be the inevitable and eternal 'number two' in any management team, a secretary must also be an independent thinker, intelligent, creative and capable of exercising considerable management skills in her own right.

The main problem is perhaps one of image. If the public perceive secretarial work to be 'women's' work (and consequently not of a professional standing) it's no wonder that so few men are willing to give it a try. Juliet Hepburn feels that radical steps must be taken to improve its public image and the potential for career development: 'We have a responsibility to secretaries to enable them to get more from what is potentially an extremely rewarding and fulfilling career.'

2

The Secretary at Work

The real essence of secretarial work is diversity. Though the basic skills and expertise may remain constant, the ways in which they are applied will vary greatly from job to job and industry to industry. It's difficult to think of many points of similarity between the job of, say, a GP's secretary and a political PA, yet both would staunchly defend their right to call themselves secretaries. The lack of any national definition has, up to now, meant that all manner of lesser clerical staff have usurped the title and in our opinion devalued it.

Because of this uncertainty about what a secretary is, grading has become an important issue in many private and public sector organizations. Without effective grading it's impossible to draw comparisons between the status of different members of staff, and resentment almost always follows. On the other hand, a grading system which depends entirely upon length of service (rather than on competence or level of qualifications) soon becomes impractical and unpopular, as in many public sector organizations.

More than most other jobs, secretarial work is acutely affected by the rapid pace of technological change. According to Margaret Evans, Senior Examinations Officer (Secretarial Studies) at the London Chamber of Commerce and Industry, many employers feel that secretaries are ideally qualified and placed to take charge of new technology. It's the secretaries who find themselves presented with a pile of computer hardware and a manual and left to get on with it. Consequently it's the secretaries who filter information about the new technology through to management.

From their position of power (for knowledge is power) secretaries can effectively control the whole life of the office. Since their time is cheaper than that of their managers, why not invest them with more and more higher-grade tasks to perform, using new technology? An increasing number of secretaries are, for example, learning about desktop publishing and so moving from simple form design into a complex publicity function involving the selection of graphics as well as layout and typeface. How long before they also generate research material and copy? Some are doing so already.

Yet, more than ever, the secretary stands as a rather lonely figure within the organization. She can't be fitted comfortably into a conventional organization chart because simply drawing in a staff relationship with management ignores the complex network of informal relationships which the secretary must build with superiors and subordinates just to get the job done.

Secretaries rely heavily upon the informal structure of an organization – using the grapevine, calling in favours and so on. Yet because the secretarial grading structure often runs parallel to the line management structure, with no formal relationship between the two, the secretary's actual authority is often severely limited. Even the Chief Executive's PA can have difficulty in persuading a junior manager to obey his or her instructions – unless of course they are seen to come directly from the Chief Executive himself.

Status and grading

Secretarial gradings

Typist	Typing 30+ wpm with reasonable accuracy. Works under supervision.
Audio-typist/Shorthand-typist	Typing 40+ wpm. Shorthand 80+ wpm. Works under supervision.
Secretary	Typing 45+ wpm. Shorthand 100 wpm. Some supervision from senior secretary where appropriate.
Private Secretary	Typing 50+ wpm. Shorthand 100+ wpm. Works for middle management. More responsibility and confidential work.
Executive Secretary/Personal Assistant	Typing 60+ wpm. Shorthand 120+ wpm. Often educated to 'A' level or degree standard. Probably has at least one other language to a conversational standard – may be bilingual.

The above is a list of secretarial gradings as seen by the Royal Society of Arts, largely in terms of skills. Unfortunately it's not as simple as that. Many other organizations – IQPS, EAPS, the LCCI and so on (see pp. 121–2) – have produced definitions, but since there is as yet no national agreement about qualifications or status, no-one is obliged to abide by any 'rules'.

Most people have a vague idea that a PA is in some way superior to a secretary and takes precedence over a shorthand-typist or a WP operator, but even this elementary grading system is not always observed by employers. The lack of any restrictions on using the title 'PA' or 'secretary', combined with the need to attract staff, has produced a mass of inflated titles for jobs which demand minimal skill and experience.

At the other end of the scale some large organizations – particularly in the public sector – take grading to ridiculous extremes. Take the case of local government, where scale 1 administrative staff are not supposed to use word processors. For them to be allowed to do so would imply that they had a level of technical expertise required of scale 2 staff, so they would have a legitimate case to apply for regrading. In point of fact, almost all college leavers now have word processing skills and would very much like the chance to use them. Being effectively banned from doing so makes their work more tedious and less productive, and does nothing to improve their promotion prospects.

Wendy Syer is Personal Assistant to Sir Campbell Adamson. She's also UK Public Relations Officer of the European Association of Professional Secretaries and has campaigned strenuously for a better career structure for secretaries. But even in her own job she has encountered problems with status and grading:

> All our jobs in Abbey were re-evaluated over the last couple of years. They were going to grade all secretaries within the Society under two headings. I kicked up a stink . . . and they said, 'Sorry, that was a bit stupid. We'll go in for a more defined grading.' I put in a few sticky words about the fact that we didn't have any sort of career structure and that the younger secretaries weren't receiving any sort of training so they could have a chance of coming up and having the top job – which I think is very important. So it all went back into the melting pot . . .

Although it took almost a year, the regrading problem has now been resolved to everyone's satisfaction.

Grading at Abbey National is carried out by Hay MSL, a large recruitment consultancy, in conjunction with the Personnel Department. One of the major factors in establishing gradings is the rigorous system of appraisals which is operated on a twice-yearly basis:

We have an appraisal system for salary increases because we're given an increase dependent on our efficiency. We have to be graded by our bosses twice a year (interim and final assessment). (. . .) Each person has objectives agreed by the boss at the beginning of the year. He flags up the faults that you should be working on, the areas you could improve. (. . .) We're graded on how we complete those objectives.

This may sound like a fairly sensible, if nerve-racking, way to maintain standards and reward excellence, but are there any drawbacks? Wendy Syer observes that although secretaries were expected to participate fully in evaluations and appraisals, they weren't treated in the same way as the rest of the workforce:

It was interesting, because when these evaluations and assessments were mooted, everyone else in the company was taught, literally, by a team of personnel people how to tackle the assessment forms – how to define your objectives, how to give your side of the story, etc., etc. The one group who were totally unbriefed were secretaries. No-one thought you'd have to teach secretaries how to do this. Whether it was a back-handed compliment or not, I don't know.

The overwhelming trend in the world of work today is towards evaluating different jobs against each other, so that some form of coherent grading and salary structure can be worked out. A case at Cammell Lairds (the shipbuilders) a couple of years ago provoked a revolution in employment legislation when a female cook successfully claimed pay parity with her male colleagues working in engineering trades. Does this mean that secretaries will soon be able to claim parity with their non-secretarial colleagues in industry, commerce and the public sector?

That's certainly the intention of the National Council for Vocational Qualifications (NCVQ). When National Vocational

Qualifications are fully implemented in the 1990s, secretaries should no longer be widely expected to take their status from that of their bosses. Grading should, at least in theory, be associated with the secretary's own level of qualification and training. The possession of NVQ level 3 or above in Business Administration will justify the use of the title 'secretary'. Below this level, it's felt that employees would be lacking in the necessary knowledge, skills and experience to merit what is really a professional title.

If the scheme works (and it's receiving full support from central Government and the TUC) we may well see the rehabilitation of the title 'secretary'. Those who have taken the time and trouble to obtain NVQs will guard their professional status jealously and will be justified in demanding a salary which reflects that status. This means that it won't be in the interests of employers to allow under-qualified or inexperienced staff to use a title which might also allow them to claim a 'secretarial' salary.

On the other hand, some doubts have been expressed about the willingness of employers to pay the proper salary for qualified secretarial staff. Why not simply employ clerical staff qualified below NVQ level 3 and then train them in the specific higher-level skills they need to do the job in question? That way the employer wouldn't have to designate the post 'secretarial' and the salary would be accordingly lower. It's also intriguing to speculate upon the reaction of, say, a boss who is qualified to NVQ level 3, to a request from his secretary to study for level 4!

Another concern is that as training becomes more work-based employers will gain more and more control over their employees' career progression. Training for higher-level NVQs will require the co-operation of employers. But why should they encourage office workers to study for qualifications which might entitle them to demand higher pay? Margaret Evans (Senior Examinations Officer at the LCCI) maintains:

> The higher up you get, you've really got to have . . . a supportive employer. Or the college that you go to to get the training has got to have a very good relationship with a local employer in order to allow a complete stranger to come in and do this high-level work. In order to satisfy some of the requirements at level 4 . . . someone is going to have to give you access to a Board meeting and they simply aren't going to do it. So that's why I say employers are going to have quite a lot of control.

It's to be hoped that NVQs will at least make organizations think harder about the sort of training opportunities and career structure which they should be providing for their secretaries. The present situation is patchy at best, with some employers happy to send their secretaries on courses that will enhance their career prospects, and others who seem to think that because they're secretaries they've no right to have ambitions. Wendy Syer notes:

> At Abbey they will help you get out of a secretarial job but they don't help young secretaries progress through the company and at the moment I'm trying to get some sort of training syllabus laid down. For branch managers, assistant branch managers, area branch managers, a list of the training courses available is published at the beginning of each year, so you could say that this year you will do this and this. But for secretaries – absolutely nothing.

Purchasing power

Whatever their official status may be within an organization, secretaries have steadily increased their power as office consumers. Isabella Szredzki (PR Officer for Alfred Marks) notes: 'As shown by the London Secretary Show, they are seen as major clients for suppliers. They are being wooed by anyone from the makers of photocopiers to the makers of typing fluid.'

This is no exaggeration. According to a 1987 survey by PEL Communications, secretaries have a collective spending power in excess of £1bn per year. Around 80% of secretaries are responsible for choosing hotels, conference venues and theatres used by their bosses, and 69% have control over the boss's travel arrangements. Many also have a say in office refurbishment and decor.

John Whittle is the publisher of *Office Secretary*, a highly successful magazine targeted at those secretaries who really do have control over the office purse-strings. It is packed with advertising and short, informative articles mainly sponsored by the advertisers. Although clearly directed at a female readership, the magazine's content is surprisingly wide-ranging. Articles on dress, cosmetics, slimming products and sexism are balanced by hard-sell, glossy promotions for photocopiers, fax machines, hygiene equipment, air conditioning and the latest in office hardware and business packages. A liberal sprinkling of general interest articles, competitions and special offers ensures that the reader sticks with the magazine right to the last page. John Whittle observed: 'We expected to carry ads for things like cosmetics, employment agencies and coffee companies. We never imagined that airlines, business system manufacturers and stationery companies would use the medium.'

Office Secretary is not alone. *Office Equipment News* and *Office Magazine* are just two of its numerous competitors in the race to benefit from secretarial spending power. Some companies have gone even further in an attempt to tap this huge potential market. Jack Gordon of Wiggins Teape Stationery comments: 'We have re-designed some products so that they're more attractive and accessible for secretaries.' With more and more companies joining the race there's every sign that this trend will continue. The London Secretary Show alone is proof of that. So secretaries can continue to enjoy a degree of influence which they wouldn't have dreamt of even ten years ago.

The secretary as boss

With the current high profile of the secretary, there's much talk about progression from secretarial work into management. In fact most secretaries are managers already. They have to deal daily with problems of time, money, information and people which many of their own managers would be unable to solve.

A new breed of secretary is now emerging: the secretary who supervises other secretarial or clerical staff on a regular basis. We're not talking about typing pool or WP supervisors (who need not be trained secretaries) but about those senior secretaries or PAs whose workload is so heavy that they need the services of other staff to help them cope with it. A survey published by the Industrial Society in 1987 entitled *Secretaries: a wasted asset?* revealed that around 22% of secretaries now supervise other employees. Most have only one person reporting to them, but 12% supervise more than five people.

As a result quite a few secretaries are finding for the first time that they are in the position of being both a subordinate and a superior. For example, the PA to a company Chairman may supervise one or two junior secretaries within the Chairman's office. This may in a sense add to status but it also increases responsibility and stress. It can lead to resentment among other secretaries who have not been quite so successful. In view of the formidable problems which have to be dealt with by human resource managers, there must surely be a good case for giving all secretaries some formal training in the basic skills of management.

Do secretaries make good bosses? Wendy Syer feels that they may even perform the job better than professional managers: 'They run much tighter ships, and they'd be much better at dealing with people . . . because that's part and parcel of what our training is about: looking after people. Whereas some (managers) have never been taught how to prioritize their papers or how to deal with members of the public.'

The secretary's working environment

Offices have changed considerably over the past few years. Gone are the typing pools, most of the typewriters, and many of the old routines. There are more open-plan or 'landscaped' offices than ever before, and large numbers of secretaries have been obliged to leave their cosy little 'cellular' offices for desks in vast and rather impersonal rooms full of employees of every conceivable grade and occupation. Some people like open-plan offices because they are more 'sociable'. Others hate them because they are noisy and don't confer the same status as a nice personal office with a nameplate on the door.

The biggest change of all is the advent of new technology on a massive scale. A secretary returning to work after a ten-year break would be completely lost among today's automated systems and integrated workstations.

The science of ergonomics and all the latest developments in safety techniques have been applied to the design of Western hi-tech offices. Yet still people complain about them: everything from a stiff neck to a miscarriage is blamed on 'the VDU', the air conditioning or the height of a typist's chair. So why do we turn technology into a scapegoat? Is it really friend or foe?

Sensitively used, the word processor and the many business software packages which are now available can enable the senior secretary to perform her real function of assisting management. Isabella Szredzki says:

With new technology there is more time available (. . .). The computer is responsible for enlarging the scope of a secretary's job if used properly (. . .). A secretary could function as a research assistant because she is researching information through databases. She can also do budget projections by using spreadsheets (. . .). By using desktop publishing she's using graphics a lot more and producing in-house newsletters – actually deciding how to design reports instead of typing them out as they were presented.

Most experts agree that the days of the humble typist are over. According to Val Tyler, 'the days of the copy typist, the filing clerk and the data entry department are numbered . . . but the secretary has a key role in most "office of the future" scenarios . . . with much of the drudgery of handling correspondence and doing the filing removed by automation' (*Word Processor International*, Spring 1987).

Now that computer training is an essential part of the school curriculum, we are rearing a 'keyboard generation'. Indeed, it is estimated that by 1991 78% of senior and middle management will have had some formal or informal training on a computer keyboard. Many managers in the future may prefer to input their own data and deal with their own correspondence, so that the large amount of routine typing and filing which is currently part of the secretary's job may become a thing of the past.

Younger employees who are familiar with word processors derive a far greater degree of job satisfaction from using them than do employees in older age groups. A Nielsen survey commissioned by Reed Employment in 1987 revealed that two-thirds of all staff who used word processors found that they made their work more interesting. The proportion increased among younger staff and it was found that a remarkable 92% of 16–17 year-olds liked working with word processors.

People who have never used a word processor tend to believe that a high level of skill is needed to operate one. In fact most modern software is very user-friendly, allowing any one of dozens of complex operations – such as centring, moving and editing text, spell-checking and justification of margins – to be performed at the push of a button. For an inexperienced typist the word processor is a gift from the gods; mistakes can be corrected before anything is printed out. Long gone are the days of the typing eraser and the bottle of congealed Tipp-Ex.

Perhaps the reason why young people work so happily with modern technology is that basic operations require so little skill. But not everyone would regard office automation as a blessing. Whilst some of the drudgery of office routine has been removed, the loss of skills can lead to a lack of variety and reduced job satisfaction.

Since the introduction of widespread office automation, studies have indicated that there are now far higher levels of stress and stress-related illness among office workers. One of the most revealing studies of recent years is discussed in a research paper by Howard Kahn and Cary Cooper entitled 'Computing Stress' and published in *Current Psychological Research and Reviews* (Summer 1986). The authors isolated no fewer than twenty-three possible causes of stress among people working with computers and VDUs:

- job (dis)satisfaction
- (un)demanding work
- worry about possible physical effects
- quality of training
- work ergonomics
- (no) social interaction with colleagues
- the 'newness' effect
- relationships with the originators of text
- career development
- role clarity
- supervisors' attitudes
- participation in job design
- work overload/underload
- job/role changes
- feedback and control over the job
- hours worked at a stretch, and in total
- variety of tasks carried out
- customer contact
- age and sex of operator
- breakdown of the machine
- clerical and professional VDU workers
- monitoring of performance
- after-work problems

Most secretaries will obviously not experience such high stress levels as those who work solely at a word processor or computer terminal, but many may experience some stress or work overload as a result of office automation. This may come as a surprise to those, including management, who imagine that automation will always make office work easier and more pleasant.

Stress often arises because new technology is imposed on old systems of working and old attitudes or because of an abrupt transition for which employees are ill-prepared. Inappropriate choices of system or software inevitably lead to frustration. It may take hours to perform a simple function which would have taken only a few seconds with the right software. There's always a danger that an inexperienced management with little specialist knowledge will buy equipment which isn't really suitable for secretarial needs, simply through a lack of consultation.

Lack of training is another common stress factor. A Manpower Services Commission study in 1981 found that it takes three months for an experienced typist to become a competent WP operator. Yet smaller firms with a limited IT budget may be reluctant to pay to send their secretaries on training courses when new systems are installed. Being presented with a boxed word processor and an incomprehensible manual is not the best way to learn about the joys of word processing! Even those firms which do make an attempt to train staff often only provide in-house courses of perhaps two or three days: enough to instill the basics, perhaps, but surely not enough to create confidence and enthusiasm.

Lack of knowledge, consultation and the feeling of having new technology imposed from above are factors which are bound to cause resentment and suspicion among secretaries, particularly in older women who may feel that their entire working life is being turned inside out by new equipment and procedures. The BBC's consumer programme *Watchdog* (23 January 1989) has revealed the extent to which office staff worry about the physical effects of radiation from VDUs. So concerned are many VDU operators that they have demanded that their firms buy protective clothing for them, even though there is no evidence that any such precautions are needed. Trade Unions and professional associations have also joined the debate. Perhaps the problem is less about physical safety than about wanting to be treated with consideration.

Dr Susan Vinnicombe and Dr Nina Colwill have outlined the problem clearly:

> New technology has clearly revitalized many secretaries' jobs. Where this has happened, it appears to be linked to management's positive attitudes towards their secretaries. They have actively involved them in planning and implementing the new technology and applying it to their jobs. On the other hand, if managers do not involve secretaries in introducing new technology and retain rigid attitudes about the manager's tasks and the secretary's tasks, then the secretary will not benefit from new technology. Her job may well deteriorate into a permanently routine typing job where she works for an increasing number of managers. ('Putting secretaries in their place', *International Management Development Review*, Corporate Strategy Management Centre, Brussels, 1988).

A fair deal at work?

Secretaries are not highly unionized, and even the membership of professional organizations like IQPS and EAPS represents only a tiny proportion of the secretarial workforce.

Because of the 'scattered' nature of secretarial work, it's not easy to create a collective consciousness or work together for the general good of the profession. It would certainly be impossible to organize an effective strike and it's doubtful whether many secretaries would be interested anyway.

So who looks after the interests of secretaries at work? Those working in the public sector are the most willing to join a Trade Union: COHSE, NUPE and NALGO being the most popular choices. Public sector employees are all subject to inflexible working conditions and this may account for a greater tendency to work together for improvements. Individuals have no chance of negotiating a pay rise, but with the collective might of a national union behind them, they have a chance. On the other hand, secretaries working in the private sector may well find their interests best served by negotiating as individuals; bosses do not like to lose really good secretaries and will offer the best pay incentives they can in order to keep them.

Outside the framework of traditional unionization there exist professional organizations which work more generally to promote the status and career prospects of secretaries and to create a professional standard through membership restrictions. They also often fulfil a social function, offering a place where secretaries can meet and discuss subjects of mutual interest. They aren't recruitment agencies but it can't be denied that they sometimes help their members to find jobs through the 'grapevine' mechanism. A list of such professional organizations is given at the end of this book.

The experts

It's probably true to say that all secretaries are experts. First, they've chosen to train as specialist administrators; second, since no two secretarial jobs are alike, each individual secretary will become an expert in his or her own job over a period of time.

However, within the specialist field of secretarial administration there's plenty of room for those who have chosen to specialize still further. Some – like those working in the financial or political sectors – may have gained most of their knowledge through on-the-job experience rather than by study. Most – the legal, medical, agricultural and bilingual specialists – have taken one or more courses to secure the job they want.

Is specialization worth it in terms of money and status? There are certainly some opportunities for financial reward. An article in the *Daily Mail* (7 February 1989) reported that salaries for legal secretaries in London averaged £13,000, with overtime rates running at around £18 per hour. The financial sector also pays well, perhaps partly because it's still a relatively unpopular destination for secretarial college leavers; and a good freelance farm secretary with an established list of clients is assured of a steady income.

'Euro-secretaries' in Brussels or Strasbourg often find that they can't afford to come back to England because they would have to take a big drop in salary and standard of living. This is an unfortunate state of affairs since many of them find life as expatriates rather dull once the novelty has worn off. One former secretary at the Council of Europe explained in the London *Evening Standard* (1 April 1985): 'Living abroad is like living in a bubble (. . .). You have got the material things but in human terms the quality of life is missing.'

To make matters worse, high salaries are not the norm for

secretarial specialists. Many bilingual and medical secretaries are particularly poorly paid, considering their level of qualifications and commitment. Money isn't everything of course, but it takes an exceptional type of person consciously to choose an area of work which requires hard work and extra study with little prospect of appropriate remuneration.

Prospects, too, are at best variable. It's admittedly not unheard of for a legal secretary to become a legal executive or even a solicitor; and MPs' secretaries have been known to become parliamentary candidates. But most specialists will begin and end their careers in secretarial work. So why do they do it, when they could earn more money in general secretarial work? The answer is that it's becoming more and more difficult to find people willing to work in the most poorly-paid specialisms.

A chronic lack of funds in the public sector means that Health Authorities have difficulty in attracting and retaining qualified secretarial staff. Secretarial work tends to be divided among a vast and ever-changing population of temps. This may be good news for the temps (who can earn a much better hourly rate than their permanent colleagues) but it's not at all popular among consultants and their staff because of the lack of continuity.

The opportunities for flexible and part-time working hours have meant that among the growing population of temps there is a liberal sprinkling of women returners: mature women returning to secretarial work after bringing up a family. Ruth Cocksedge works in the Paediatric Department of a major London teaching hospital as a secretary on the Higher Clerical Officer grade. Her work is part-time, and she took the job when her elder child reached school age. She started work at the hospital as a temp with few paper qualifications. She explains: 'I've always been interested in medical work because I did train to be a nurse for a while, so for me, it wasn't difficult (. . .). The main reward of the job is knowing that you are helping the children.'

Ruth's work involves typing reports to the Court in child abuse cases and related medical correspondence. Needless to say, this can be very harrowing:

The job is not stressful so much as frustrating. When I read the reports about the children I wish I could go out and strangle the parents. The job can be emotionally draining. You have to try to remain detached, but sometimes you get the same child's name appearing again and again and again – you almost know the child – and then I think it gets a bit wearing.

Specialist secretarial work requires special people: secretaries who have dedication and a clear idea of what they want to do. For most of them job satisfaction comes way ahead of money in terms of priorities – but isn't it time we recognized their worth and started to pay them accordingly?

The best man for the job?

Judging from secretarial magazines, jokes, cartoons, newspaper articles and situation comedies, it would be easy to conclude that secretarial work is, was and always will be a female profession. After all, what self-respecting male would allow himself to be patted on the head and referred to as the 'office wife'?

Surprisingly enough, Reed Employment reported in February 1989 that one in every twenty prospective secretarial recruits they interview is male. This is really nothing new. A hundred years ago, secretarial work was an almost exclusively male occupation; it meant an important and confidential position which it was widely believed could never be entrusted to a mere woman. A century later men are thinking seriously about reclaiming their inheritance.

Female secretaries are very much aware of the trend and not everyone is happy about it:

> Look at the City. The City is classic. The City is full of PAs – real PAs – and they're men. Many of the people who are closest to the captains of industry are men. Plucked out of University, I should think. They write the speeches, they stand in, they do research and, in fact, you will find that a lot of the very senior secretaries in the City are pretty cheesed off sometimes, because all the interesting bits are men's. (J. Hepburn, Industrial Society)

As if to bear out this theory the *Daily Mail* (21 February 1989) published an article entitled 'Mr Super-Secretary' and announced: 'He earns £35,000 because of his skill with the computer.' According to this article men are taking a new route to the top of the business world by working as high-flying 'sec-execs' whose winning combination of secretarial and computing skills gives them *carte blanche* to name their salary.

One of the new breed of male high-fliers is Geoff Payne, who works for Mrs Caroline Black (one of the directors of VandenBurg Associates – a major West End PR agency). Interestingly his boss says that 'he is so computer literate that he brings the sort of experience I've never found in any of our girls.'

Why should this be? Why are women in danger of missing out on these phenomenal salaries? Is it a question of some inherent masculine ability in micro-technology or perhaps more a question of education and upbringing? Surely women ought to be ideally placed to continue their dominance of the secretarial job market at this time of rapid change and maximum opportunity. Yet employers seem happy to take advantage of the new male willingness to step into technology-based secretarial posts. Pauline Kent (account manager for Reed) comments: 'A man who is unhappy being behind a typewriter is happy with a computer because he has a much more macho image.'

One could be forgiven for thinking that since computing is now an integral part of the school curriculum for junior level upwards, girls and boys ought to be equally at home with developments in new technology. If girls really are as competent and as interested in this area as men, then employers may not be giving them the opportunity to prove it. Whether this is the result of discrimination or of male applicants' superior technological background is difficult to say.

Most female secretaries welcome the return of men to the profession, believing that their presence can only force salaries up and improve the status of the job, as has happened in nursing. On the other hand, there are still worries that once established, men will take all the best jobs. Charles Windsor, PA to the Managing Director of Faulkner Studios, made the following reassuring observation: 'You ask any boss who they think is the most important person in a company and they'll say "the secretary". Nine times out of ten the secretary is, of course, female' *(Today's PA*, 8 June 1988).

This may be the case today: but who can say what the situation will be in ten years' time?

Top teams?

Secretarial work can be challenging, enjoyable and sometimes even glamorous. But few 'ordinary' jobs can match the excitement of working for a well-known public figure – or so one might imagine. We have all wondered from time to time how famous people acquire their secretarial staff. Mrs Thatcher doesn't seem to make much use of Office Angels or the local Job Centre!

Liz Aydon has worked as secretary to *Watership Down* author Richard Adams for the last six years. She is a qualified Legal Executive and had no thought of leaving the Law until the day when Richard walked into her office looking for someone to type a letter. From typing the occasional letter Liz progressed to sorting out Richard's fan mail, and after a while he asked her if she would like to work for him on a full-time basis. After careful consideration and prayer (she's a committed Christian) Liz accepted. As Mr Adams points out: 'There was no question of interviewing her for the job – there weren't a number of applicants. She fell in my way, if you like, and fortunately we found we got on very well together.'

When she left school Liz had every intention of becoming an actress. But her mother's concern that she should have 'something to fall back on' led Liz into a one-year secretarial course at her local Technical College, which, to her surprise, she enjoyed. After qualifying Liz went on to work in shipbuilding and papermill plants and factories as a secretary before going into the Air Force, where she met her first husband. The break-up of her first marriage brought with it the necessity to earn a living and Liz returned to work in a local firm of solicitors – first as a secretary and then as a Legal Executive. She remained there for seventeen years, until her chance meeting with Richard Adams.

Richard Adams considers himself a demanding employer: 'I don't make any concessions at all. Although we're great friends, if Liz makes a mistake I'm on it like a knife.' This could be due to his experience of secretaries during his twenty-five years as a Civil Servant:

All the secretaries you got when I was a Civil Servant at that level (Assistant Secretary) tended to have something the matter with them, so they couldn't command a full salary outside. Miss A was a very nice woman, but very prone to get sick: she'd go over in a puff of wind. If you got a fraught afternoon with half a dozen

Parliamentary questions and something the Under Secretary wanted in a hurry, you could bet your boots that Miss A would be ill the following morning. I think it was perfectly genuine. She was just very fragile. Then I had a Mrs B, whom I was rather fond of. She had been in a mental hospital and was very strange in her ways. She was a good typist and very good on the telephone – she gave a very good first impression. It wasn't until you got to know her that you realized that she definitely wasn't quite all there. Those were the sort of secretaries you had in the Civil Service – and of course, they weren't yours personally. They could go at five o'clock.

Richard's experience with Liz has been very different. He was delighted to find that she not only possessed excellent secretarial skills but was also extremely well-read: 'She doesn't often make a mistake. Sometimes we find ourselves having a friendly bet on how you spell something and she nearly always wins. Liz is literate, which is a great help (. . .). Usually I don't have to explain anything.'

Liz's job is far removed from the nine-to-five office routine. As Richard points out:

It's a very variable job. Sometimes there really isn't a great deal to do. But at other times there's frantic activity – such as when a novel is being typed in its final form to go to the publisher or something has to be retyped in a hurry and sent out. . . . You never know when there are going to be letters requiring an urgent reply. Liz hardly ever has to do shorthand because she can type about as fast as I can dictate. I dictate straight onto the typewriter.

Yet he admits that it's a leisurely life compared with the Civil Service.

I can't think of any swift decision that would have to be made in my absence. Sometimes Liz replies to letters on her own account because we get an awful lot of fan mail, sometimes from children, sometimes from adults, sometimes even in languages that we don't understand. It's my policy to reply to all fan letters. I reckon you're only as good as your fans make you.

Liz agrees. 'We try to put ourselves in the recipient's shoes. They've taken the trouble to write and therefore I believe they deserve the courtesy of a reply, even if it's "I'm sorry, but no."'

One of the things Liz likes about her job is the variety. No two days are the same:

> Mostly I will come into the Library and if there's filing to do I generally do it. If there are any fan letters that I am going to answer, I get them done while Mr Adams is doing something else, like writing some more book or whatever. Then we might have a letter session, or it might be copy typing or photocopying. You can't really say any day is the same because it isn't. It's one of the things I love about it. Basically I'm employed from ten till five, but I'm quite happy to come in early or work a bit later if the occasion arises, and I'm very fortunate in that if Mr Adams doesn't require me any more for that day I can go home.

Liz's most important task is to help with the preparation of Richard's manuscripts. This is a painstaking procedure, demanding great patience and accuracy. Richard says:

> The way we work is that I write in longhand. Liz will get it back and I generally cut the first draft to pieces. The second draft gets a bit better but it's still corrected. I get it in double-space and chop it about. And we go on until we're satisfied really. Some passages have been retyped eight times until I got what I wanted – out of my own head, I mean.

Surprisingly, neither Richard nor Liz uses a word processor. Richard explains:

> I never type anything, so the word processor would be used by Liz, and she's not frightfully struck with the idea. If she wanted a word processor she could have one, but so far our researches into the subject haven't motivated us. I must confess that they strike me as rather impersonal things. I think that I should feel my work was getting machine-made somehow.

One area which gives them both great satisfaction is their animal rights work. Richard Adams is a tireless anti-fur-trade campaigner

32

and Liz shares his enthusiasm, a fact which he considers very important. 'My previous secretary could never see the point: she thought it was a total waste of time. And the result was that when you gave her anything about the animals you felt, "Oh Lord – I know she isn't going to enjoy this, and probably wishes she could go home." Liz, you see, shares a common feeling with me for the animals and that helps a lot.'

The relationship between boss and secretary is close, personal and symbiotic. Liz is much more than a typist – she helps to eliminate inconsistencies of plot and detail from Richard's work and even makes suggestions for improving the text. She's also not above making the odd shopping trip or even recruiting her husband to help move a consignment of coal! In fact, Richard describes her as 'an honorary member of the family'. As Liz says: 'We communicate very well and Mr Adams is the closest employer I've ever had. . . . Here, I feel we're working as a team, which I like very much. It's like a partnership.'

Richard's most recent book was *Traveller*, a novel about the American Civil War. Writing it proved immensely stressful for him and this is where the trust which he had built up with Liz came to the fore. 'When you dwell in your imagination day after day upon that war it affects you. After some months I was suffering from a really bad depression – well, Liz was very helpful over that. You need someone you like and trust. If you come in here in a dressing gown crying, you need someone who understands.'

We asked Richard what he believed a secretary's function was. He pointed to the traditional skills of shorthand and typing but also adds that he expected his secretary to be 'a sort of second memory' –someone whose filing is exemplary and who never forgets a face or a name. Liz agreed but went further: 'A secretary should feel that she is supporting her employer in every way that will help his career and look out for things that need to be done without having to be asked.' They both felt that a successful boss/secretary team hinges upon a respect for each other's professional competence, flexibility and a genuine liking for each other.

In spite of the high value which he places upon his secretary, Richard nevertheless doesn't believe that secretarial work is a career. 'It isn't a career, is it? There's no career grade really. I mean, you don't get promoted from Secretary grade 3 to Secretary grade 2 to Secretary grade 1. Too often I think you'll find the secretary who's grown grey in the boss's service. We try to ensure that Liz's salary keeps pace with inflation at least, and to bump it up a bit from time to time.' For her part Liz feels amply compensated for any lack of career structure. 'I've got so much personal freedom timewise, and the Adamses are very generous – feed and water me and so on. The word "status" doesn't really enter my mind. It's just a lovely job, in a lovely place.'

Annalisa Hamilton moves in a very different world: the world of the Boardroom and multi-million-pound decisions. As Assistant to Sir Terence Conran, Annalisa is at the top of the secretarial tree and at the very centre of activity in Storehouse plc – the giant retail group which includes famous names like Habitat, Mothercare and British Home Stores.

When Annalisa was telephoned by recruitment consultant Judy Farquharson, who 'head-hunted' her for the vacant post, she was surprised and pleased: 'From my point of view I was a "Habitat baby" by age and had followed Sir Terence's career and knew what his interests were – so I was very interested.'

Sir Terence had delegated the initial interviews to his outgoing PA, because 'she would know better than I what I needed'. He did admit that he was looking for 'someone who was experienced, had a mature outlook and a good sense of humour – someone who was interested in the sort of work I do.' He was also looking for a candidate who was both numerate and had a knowledge of French.

Besides Annalisa, two other members of staff help in the running of Sir Terence's office: a secretary and a driver. Sir Terence also employs two other part-time secretaries outside Storehouse to help him with his other business interests, which he describes as 'considerable and diverse'. These interests range from restaurants and property development to writing and design consultancy and an architectural practice.

Annalisa sees herself as the bridge between Sir Terence and his many business interests. She makes sure that none of his activities and meetings overlap and that everything slots together 'like a jigsaw'. Sir Terence admits: 'My diary is a nightmare to organize – getting all these meetings in, going abroad a lot, doing a lot of travel; quite a large part of Annalisa's job is to see that I'm in the right place at the right time and to see that my driver can get me there.'

In spite of all her boss's travel Annalisa never accompanies Sir Terence on his business trips. He believes that her function is to ensure the smooth running of the office in his absence. This involves a considerable amount of delegation and trust. Sir Terence continues: 'We have the sort of relationship where she would know how far to go without asking me about something. Obviously, over a period of time, your confidence grows.'

Working under considerable pressure means that Annalisa has to have sufficient confidence in her colleagues to be able to delegate work to them as well. 'There has to be a fairly wide overlap between roles. You can't say "that's where my responsibility ends."'

Sir Terence admits to an 'open' style of management, and his office is always open to members of his own organization who wish to talk to him. On the other hand he relies upon Annalisa to be a barrier between him and those people outside the organization (e.g. the press) whom he would rather not talk to. Annalisa says: 'I need the ability to prevaricate in the nicest possible way and sometimes in the nastiest possible way! There are times when you say, "you really shouldn't be coming back to me for the fourth time on this, Buster."' Sir Terence agrees. 'The secretary has to be the "fence" to allow me to pick up the pieces later – a sort of "Mutt and Jeff" act. I can be nice and Annalisa will take all the flak.'

Annalisa's boss has a great deal of confidence in her management skills and believes that many high-level PAs could successfully run their own businesses 'because they've seen the process of management. They understand how the business is run, what the priorities are in business and how the boss deals with certain situations. They could learn far more than they'd ever pick up at business school.' Yet when asked whether he would be happy for his own assistant to train as a manager, his reply was blunt and to the point: 'Certainly not! She's far too important doing all the bits and pieces. I'd be lost without her.'

For all Sir Terence's unwillingness to part with his assistant, Annalisa has the sort of experience which would be very valuable in retail management. In fact it's a recognized career progression to move from being PA to the Chairman or Chief Executive to being a junior manager with brilliant career prospects. To quote Annalisa: 'There are very few jobs like mine for women – mainly they are held by men who subsequently fit easily into the management structure.' Sir Terence adds that male PAs are generally recruited straight from business school rather than via any secretarial route.

Like many secretaries and PAs working for public figures, Annalisa Hamilton does not regard her work as glamorous: 'I hate that word being used, because it means people don't actually understand what I'm talking about. You could call it great fun, and you do meet interesting people, but other people obviously think your life is filled with parties or something.' Sir Terence agrees: 'It's extremely hard work and very demanding.'

Annalisa likes to keep her home life and her business life separate: 'Taking work home is the one thing I won't do. I'd rather stay here till 8.30 or 9 o'clock until the work is done. Otherwise, when you get home you find you've brought the office with you.'

Like Liz Aydon Annalisa Hamilton has the greatest respect and liking for her boss: 'I don't see how you could work for someone you don't like. It's a very close working relationship.' She takes any attack on Sir Terence as a personal insult. 'It took me many years to pick up Sir Terence's ability not to react when I thought he'd been unfairly treated by the press. I used to go into orbit about some of the things that had been written and I wanted to shout at the journalist who'd written it.'

Sir Terence draws parallels between the working relationship and marriage. Although Annalisa does not altogether agree with this, she does admit that there are some similarities in terms of give and take. What we have noticed above all in talking to Liz and Annalisa is the extent to which they empathize with their bosses and seek (consciously or otherwise) to protect them from harsh publicity and the glare of public scrutiny.

Annalisa thinks that one day, after her son has finished his education, she might venture out from the security of secretarial work and start her own business. Perhaps one day Liz Aydon will return to the Law. Who knows? But for the time being both seem to have found their 'perfect' secretarial jobs.

3

The Agency Game

Agencies and temps

A decade ago, being a temp meant being out of work: filling in and doing all the jobs no-one else wanted to do, like three months' worth of filing or trying to reduce a photocopying mountain of EEC proportions.

Why temp?

The answers to this question are all around us. It's almost impossible to avoid the huge volume of agency 'propaganda', whether you're travelling to work, listening to commercial radio, reading a newspaper or watching television. The message comes across loud and clear: being a temp is upmarket and fun.

Temping is now considered by many to be a career, and career temps are careful to proclaim pride in their work; they arrive on time, they seldom make mistakes, they're organized . . . and they're professional. The agency advertisements are aimed as much at potential employers as at the temps themselves. The overall result is an increased public awareness of temps and a noticeable rise in status.

Being a temp is no longer a Cinderella job. It's now advertised as a high-profile, lucrative career, capable of funding an enviable lifestyle. Temping can supply a fat wage packet plus plenty of free time in which to spend it. Many advertisements carry glossy pictures of temps relaxing on beaches or lounging by swimming pools ('get out of the pool and into the pool'). Ordinary secretaries drink white wine; temps apparently drink huge and extravagant cocktails laden with cherries and lettuce leaves. One advertisement shows a secretary drawing a picture of the Rialto in Venice and is captioned: 'Freedom to draw more than a salary'.

The big recruitment agencies are spending millions of pounds on hard-sell advertising and PR, all to persuade anyone who is vaguely dissatisfied with his or her job that temping is the answer. Where else can you find such exciting jobs, such variety, such good pay, such flexibility? It appears to be money well spent. According to a recent Reed survey, 60% of employers now see temping as a career.

One of the new breed of temps is Joanna Bright who, between acting jobs, temps for Alfred Marks. 'Temping is perfect for me. I hate doing nothing, staying in all day; but also I could never take a permanent secretarial job. As it is I can go for auditions, take time off for filming, keep busy and keep earning. I'll carry on until I've got so many acting jobs that there's no time' (*Powerhouse*, Alfred Marks' house magazine, Spring 1988).

The success of temping is bound up with the cult of the individual. You can temp whilst making the contacts to set up your own business, developing your career on the stage or even studying part-time for another career. The pages of the recruitment agencies' free magazines are full of such success stories. Temping is the buccaneering spirit of free enterprise – typical of today's young entrepreneur in the making – and it's also much more acceptable than drawing social security and waiting for something to turn up!

As the spectre of unemployment has faded somewhat over the last few years, at least in the South East, far fewer people have felt the need to remain in a dead-end job just for the sake of security. Increasingly temping is viewed as a way of earning more money and enjoying a bit of variety at the same time. Of course agencies have to persuade would-be temps that they can deliver the goods, that it's not going to mean a succession of boring typing jobs and that the temp will be valued and appreciated. Agencies have now succeeded in removing many of the old objections to temping such as lack of security, no sick pay and no paid holidays, by setting up in-house schemes of their own. This helps temps to feel that they're working for an 'employer' who takes care of them and does more than just supply their weekly wage packet.

Are any temps in it just for the money? According to the agencies and temps we have interviewed many temps take a serious approach to their work and have definite career objectives which they feel they can best achieve through temping. Secretaries can benefit considerably from the wider experience of working in different organizations. Their transferable skills make it relatively easy for them to adapt to any new situation. Provided that they stay with a company long enough to learn, they will gain experience which will make them more attractive to an employer and widen their job options. Many secretaries also welcome temping as a means of trying out a variety of jobs and employers to see which environment suits them best. And of course, with money and security to tempt them, there is an ever-growing band of 'career temps'.

Women returners

Temping is still one of the most popular ways for women returners to get back into the job market. However, most agency advertising is directed at the young and whilst older staff are welcome we believe that they are not adequately rewarded for their age and experience. More than that, the opportunities simply aren't there.

In their efforts to fill temporary and permanent vacancies, agencies are casting their net more widely all the time, and the major untapped source of secretarial labour are women returners – those who left full-time employment to have a family and who wish to return to work without the commitment of a full-time, permanent job. Often they feel that they've lost some of their 'speeds' or that they need updating in terms of new office technology, and here agencies can help with individual training programmes.

In spite of the efforts made by recruitment agencies to persuade them otherwise, many employers are still resistant to the idea of employing older people, especially as secretaries. Brian Spence, Joint Managing Director of Alexis Personnel, says: 'We get secretaries with three or four GCSEs and a year or two's training and we can place them at £9,000–£9,500. And yet if they come to us at, say, twenty-six, when they've got eight years' experience in a senior job and a good work record, maybe we can get them £1,500 more. It's ludicrous.' This is a trend which appears to worsen the older you get. For secretaries over forty earnings potential actually decreases.

Susan Beck of Susan Beck Recruitment tells us that her clients often ask for a top calibre secretary, but she must be twenty-five. 'You say, "Well hang on a minute – you can't have everything. A secretary of thirty-five to forty has got everything you need." You've got to educate your client to take someone older.'

A major problem for employers is the question of image. Many bosses still see the secretary as a status symbol. Although short-hand, typing and general office skills are still essential qualifications for a secretary, skills make up only 20% of what an employer is looking for. The other 80%, according to Brian Spence, consists of 'personality, dress, figure and looks. Chauvinism is alive and well and living in the West End of London. I tried to place an applicant recently. She was absolutely excellent – over forty – she looked quite young and attractive, intelligent, I phoned up one of our clients and said "I've got someone who's forty-six" and his reply was, "Provided that's her bust measurement – no problem." '

Big business

The temp business is dominated by the big high street recruitment agencies like Alfred Marks, Reed, and Brook Street (who also place permanent staff). Behind them come the smaller, often specialized, appointment bureaux and recruitment consultants. FRES (the Federation of Recruitment and Employment Specialists) lists 11,500 licensed agencies of which the vast majority are high street branches of national recruitment organizations. Their combined turnover is over £4bn and most of their income is raised from placing temporary staff.

It's the temporary job market which has seen the biggest growth in recent years. Terry Milliken, British and European Marketing Manager for Drake International, states that 'in the past five years there's been a 65% increase in the demand for temporary workers'.

During the recession, companies cut back on their office staff. New technology enabled the routine or time-consuming jobs to be done quickly, freeing staff to take on other duties. Spreadsheets took the hard work out of financial calculations and word processing software meant that routine letters could be stored in a computer's memory and reproduced or adapted at will. Mailmerge could combine names and addresses with a standard template and so produce huge numbers of personalized letters on demand. Typing pools became a thing of the past.

For the secretary this was an important time because the job became both more varied and more demanding. According to Isabella Szredzki of Alfred Marks, 'As a result of manpower planning the secretary had to combine the roles of other members of staff. The trend was away from segmentation. Today's secretary has more administrative responsibility, is likely to undertake more research, and has more responsibility for purchasing decisions.'

Since the recession, companies have begun to expand and take on more staff; but they are more wary of advertising for permanent staff, since they now accept uncertainty over staffing levels as a way of life. Hiring temps gives them greater flexibility. Little wonder that agencies have reported their fastest-ever growth rate.

According to a Reed Employment survey published in April 1988, there are 5.6 million temps working in the UK today, a formidable proportion of the national workforce. Reed believe that by the year 2000 temps will outnumber permanent staff. But can the boom in temporary work continue to grow at its present rate? According to figures published in a Department of Employment/ NEDO report (*Young People and the Labour Market: a Challenge for the 1990s*), the number of 16 to 24-year-olds is projected to fall between 1987 and 1995 by 1.2m, a fifth of their present number. And it's these very young people who make up the pool of temporary labour.

Even now, the shortage of qualified secretaries is painfully apparent. Brian Spence (of Alexis Personnel) is finding it progressively harder to fill secretarial vacancies in central London:

At this year's FRES [the Federation of Recruitment and Employment Specialists] conference we were told there will be 30% fewer secretarial college leavers this year (1988) than last, and that the trend was likely to continue (. . .) It's unquestionably a problem area at the moment. We have a situation – especially in the centre of London – where there are fewer and fewer secretaries available for more and more jobs, and fewer and fewer secretaries wish to remain as secretaries.

The scarcity of trained secretaries has resulted in higher and higher salaries being offered in a bid to attract staff. To quote Brian Spence again, 'salaries over the past couple of years have gone through the roof.'

Far from encouraging more people to train as secretaries, the rise in salary levels has been instrumental in causing staff shortages. According to Brian Spence, 'What was happening was that a lot of people were changing jobs and this was creating severe shortages. Now companies have adjusted their secretarial salaries the movement has stopped. I don't think people are aware of the opportunities secretaries have of earning top money, otherwise we'd be seeing more college leavers.'

Staff shortages are making temps very choosy, and this has led to some rather desperate measures in an attempt to make one job appear more attractive than another. In order to try and fill vacancies for what would previously have been called typists, employers are labelling these low-grade jobs as 'secretarial'. This is not a positive move, as the title of secretary has been devalued and experienced professional secretaries have felt their status being eroded. Some agencies are having to resort to more senior-sounding job titles to attract applicants. Susan Beck gives one example:

> We get a lot of jobs in and we say, 'Call it an office manager and you'll be all right: you'll get loads of people coming.' 'But we want typing.' 'That's OK so long as you don't say there's a lot.' Office Manager: it's just a label. In the past year or so, we've all tried to think of different ways to convince applicants to at least look at a vacancy. If we feel that the client's suitable for her and that she's suitable for the client, at least it encourages her to go and look.

Choosing an agency

Choosing an agency can be a bit like entering a lottery. But at least there are plenty of prizes for the temp to win.

Most agencies now offer statutory sick pay and insurance against accidents at work. Many offer holiday pay, which is earned after a qualifying period that varies from agency to agency – 400 to 750 hours is the norm. Training, careers advice, discount on BUPA membership, membership of clubs and discount shopping schemes – the perks are many and varied.

Terms and conditions have certainly improved, but there's a purpose behind all these benefits. Some perks offer the temp a positive incentive to stay with the same agency. They are in recognition, if you like, of the temp's loyalty, demonstrating the two-way relationship between agency and temp. This is why many perks are cumulative; the holiday pay and bonuses all depend on length of service. Some agencies also reward quality through 'temp of the month' or 'temp of the year' awards for exceptional standards of work sustained over a period of time. One agency has a 'Silver Award' scheme, whereby the temp receives a silver necklace if she receives two consecutive good or excellent references from clients. Presumably the male temps receive silver cuff-links!

But the temp doesn't have it all ways. Often there's a choice to be made between continuity of employment with a moderate hourly rate and, say, short periods of employment at a higher hourly rate. Or the choice could be between intermittent interesting jobs in a prestigious sector of employment and steady but boring jobs for which the temp is frankly over-qualified. It often boils down to the relationship between the temp and the agency, or even the individual employment counsellor.

One of the complaints frequently heard from temps, particularly those who take on a succession of short-term assignments, is that they're isolated and no longer feel part of a caring organization. They belong nowhere; they're not even in contact with other temps. On the other hand, perks can encourage the temp to identify with the agency as one might identify with an employer. Many of the larger agencies now publish glossy 'house' magazines which are given free to all their staff. Besides the usual escapist fare of fashion, holidays and competitions, the magazines give information about jobs, employment trends, new training, developments within the agency and – of course – an interview with the 'temp of the month'. The magazines perform a valuable PR function.

Perhaps the greatest perk of all is personal contact. For some agencies, this means organized 'riverboat disco parties' or 'social evenings'. This may only amount to a glass of wine and a few nuts, but it's certainly an improvement on simply handing out job specs and wage slips at the end of the week. Other agencies take the matter much more seriously and offer (instead or as well) personal career counselling with advice on training needs, interview technique and self-presentation.

It's often the smaller agencies who can spare the time to get to know all their workers personally. Susan Beck believes the personal approach can pay off:

If someone comes through the door – even if we think there's no way we can place them – we still give him or her the time of day. Like . . . a gentleman came in and he was sixty-five and didn't want to retire. He said: 'Do you have any admin jobs?' Well, the only job we had which you could classify as admin was a stock controller on computers, and he didn't have the experience. So I spent some time with him and I gave him the names and addresses of charity recruitment agencies – they're more flexible to taking the older person – so that man went away happy. He may go away and tell his daughter. It's important that applicants leave with a good taste in their mouths.

What an agency does

Why call in an agency? What expertise do agencies have to offer?

When it comes to recruiting permanent office staff, many firms rely heavily on the expertise of recruitment agencies. It's not just a question of small businesses which are too busy or don't have the experience to recruit successfully. The personnel departments of large organizations often deal exclusively with one agency with whom they have always had a satisfactory relationship in the past, or alternatively may call on several agencies to draw up a shortlist of suitable candidates for interview.

Agencies can, and do, take great pains to match an applicant's skills and personality with the client's needs. Typically this will involve regular contact between client and agency, with the agency representative calling on the personnel officer or manager in person. Unlike open advertising there's a certain confidentiality in using an agency to recruit permanent staff. And of course candidates are screened by the agency before being put forward for interview, so the proportion of really unsuitable applicants should be much lower.

It's also important to bear in mind that temping is a good way for employer and employee to test each other out. And it's not at all uncommon for temporary positions to be made permanent.

What price temps?

As far as the employer is concerned, temping is all a question of supply and demand; and as demand escalates and the supply of good temps diminishes the rates charged by agencies must inevitably rise. All the agencies are locked in fierce competition for the lion's share of a limited pool of skilled labour, and hourly rates for good temporary staff have risen sharply. If employers want a skilled temp, they must be prepared to pay more per hour than they would for a permanent member of staff. Agencies can negotiate higher rates than individuals can, so it's the rule that for the same job a temp will always be paid more. Employers also pay the agency a percentage (in addition to the temp's wage) as commission, so their outlay is increased still further.

Many companies are realizing that although temps may be paid a higher weekly rate, there are considerable cost savings that make hiring temps an attractive proposition. Employers are prepared to pay more in the short term for a temp because their on-costs are practically non-existent. There's no national insurance, pension contribution, sick pay or holiday pay to consider; the temp is simply paid pro rata for the hours worked.

The indispensable temp

Changing technology, organizational changes, shifts in approach and direction of management: all these create a need for a more adaptable workforce and for the deployment of new skills. It costs money and takes time to train staff; so if agencies can supply ready-trained temps, this helps overcome a temporary skills shortage and gives the company time to train more of its permanent staff.

Nowadays the business environment is much less static. With mergers, takeovers and 'rationalization' all around us, temps are a way of ensuring continuity of work and of avoiding costly redundancy payments. Companies also tend to plan their expansion more carefully, often using temporary workers to test whether the workload is sufficient to justify taking on permanent staff. If you take on a temp and find that there's not enough work for her, or that she's simply not good enough, you can send her back to the agency without further complications. On the other hand, if she turns out to be exactly what you need, you can always offer her a permanent job. Mind you, companies who do offer permanent jobs to temps are obliged to pay the agency a percentage of her first year's salary. According to Susan Beck, 'Many employers will take them on as temporary before making them permanent, to give them a trial run.'

4

The Secretary Trap

Why is it that so many secretaries remain secretaries throughout their working lives? Why is career progression so difficult? Shouldn't it be the norm to start out as trainee secretary (grade 1), move up to secretarial co-ordinator and finish off your career as managing secretary? It sounds silly, doesn't it? In fact, most secretaries just become better secretaries.

For some firms fancy job titles are the corporate equivalent of the New Year's Honours List. Instead of pay rises, hard work and the 'right attitude' are rewarded with some new, ego-boosting job description. It's often said that the reward for being an efficient secretary is a share in your boss's glory. It's certainly true that an awful lot of secretaries view their role as a supportive one, quietly making behind-the-scenes sacrifices which enable the boss to reap the recognition and the reward for visible results.

Boss/secretary teams are built on relationships, often consisting of a 'dominant male' boss and a 'subservient female' secretary, which is no doubt why secretaries are so often described as office 'wives'. Such comparisons rightly infuriate most professional secretaries because of the attendant innuendoes. Yet it's true that many high-flying boss/secretary teams stay together for years, even decades; and in some respects a successful executive can become closer to his secretary than his wife. As the boss moves up the organization, the secretary follows; along the way she acquires intangible benefits such as her own office, freedom to organize her work, the respect of her colleagues, and so on. Top secretaries will often also receive a host of real perks, such as subsidized or free travel, expenses, a company car, BUPA, low interest mortgages and bonuses.

But in spite of all these perks, many secretaries realize that the fundamental premise of their job has not changed: someone else is still in control, someone else still takes all the credit. So why shouldn't that someone else be them?

Moving on

What makes secretaries swap their career for a new, and perhaps more demanding one? Is it some new-found confidence? Is it an ambition which has been there all along? Or have they acquired new skills and contacts through being a secretary? It could be any, all or none of these things – people are complicated. The decision to move on will probably be the result of a number of influences which come together at the same time. But you have to be able to spot opportunities and have the confidence to take the initiative. Take Lola Hatmil, for example.

Once secretary to the editor of the London Daily News, Lola Hatmil is now a journalist herself. She recalls that her earliest ambition was to be a journalist:

> When I was little, you know, when aunts and uncles came round they'd say, 'What do you want to be?' and I'd say, 'I want to be a journalist'. But that was just pie in the sky possibly. You're asked something and you give an answer.

Lola's 'O' level results were not encouraging, and she found she had an awkward career decision to make. 'I'd applied to do the London Chamber of Commerce Private Secretary's Diploma – it was all sort of high-falutin' and not me at all. I didn't fancy doing it.' But fate took a hand.

> One day, I was reading the *Evening Standard*. There was this ad the *Times* had put in saying they wanted secretarial trainees. So I applied, and twelve of us out of two hundred got in. This was September 1973, and I did typing, shorthand and office practice. I got my 100 wpm shorthand, got my advanced typing – Pitman's. The other thing was, you were paid while doing the course, like a TOPS scheme, and you were also guaranteed a job at the end of it. I worked in the Financial Advertising Department – very nice people, but I really wanted to work in Editorial. And then the chance came up to work as secretary to the Home News Desk. It was me working for ten men, trying to keep them under control – with a list of pub phone numbers in case something urgent happened and I'd have to ring round and find out where the hell they were! All in all, I was at the *Times* for about four and a half years.

But Lola's career as a secretary was about to take another turn.

I'd always liked French, and I had an idea that I would like to work in France. It's quite weird how things happen. I was sitting reading the *Times* one morning and there was an advert for secretaries for the Council of Europe at Strasbourg and I worked for the Legal Affairs Correspondent. He kept saying to me, 'Strasbourg's brilliant. You must go'. I'd been brushing up my French at evening classes and managed to get a grade B at 'O' level (I got an E in school). I was already halfway through taking an 'A' level when I was summoned by telegram for the post in Strasbourg. So off I went and I started a job which I stayed in for seven years. If you had any qualms about spending money, you know, you just forgot them. You went totally mad and bought what you wanted, when you wanted it. By the time I left in 1983 I was earning 96,000 francs tax free, about £8,000.

Lola got used to the sort of jet-setting lifestyle that many secretaries dream of. But she eventually tired of it and came back to Britain in search of pastures new. However, picking up the threads of her career was not as easy as she'd imagined.

In Britain, it didn't seem to matter that you'd spent seven years speaking French every day. There were graduate secretaries straight out of secretarial school who were going out and getting jobs as bilingual secretaries without ever having set foot in France. In the end, I decided I'd drop my languages. I'd go back into newspapers. Once loved, never forgotten. So I did. It took me a year. Again sitting reading the *Standard* one night, I saw a job as a secretary on the foreign news desk of the *Observer*. If you wanted something using languages that was the place to go. So I started in September 1984.

At the *Observer* Lola met the man with whom she was to work in close partnership, and whom she would eventually follow to the *London Daily News* when he became its Editor.

Magnus (Linklater) had started the month before me at the *Observer*. Although I wasn't his secretary we all worked for Magnus. He was Managing Editor (News). He had control of the whole News Desk – foreign and home – and he had last say on front page splashes and things. He sat opposite me. It was great. You know, what I really liked was when we were discussing headlines and Harris polls and things, and Magnus would always look at me directly and say, 'What do you think?'

I got to the stage where I wasn't treated as a secretary any more – I was respected. One night I had got home rather late and was cooking dinner. My boyfriend was sitting in the kitchen and he turned on the television. We caught the tail-end of the Thames News headline that Magnus Linklater had got the job as Editor of Maxwell's latest baby, the *London Daily News*. And I just couldn't believe my ears! Well as far as I knew, Magnus didn't have a secretary, so I thought why not ask him if he wanted one and, you know, go for it!

A short time later, Lola made Magnus an offer he couldn't refuse.

I was going on holiday to Greece so I said to Magnus, 'I won't see you when you leave. I won't be there at your drink-up. Why don't we go out for a drink?' And so we did. We went to El Vino's. And I just, you know, took a deep breath and said. 'Magnus, I've got a proposition!' He looked at me a bit askance. And I said, 'If you haven't got a secretary at the *London Daily News* I'll come along and be your secretary and do my stuff.' And we never looked back. That was it.

Or, as they say in the movies, the rest is history! But while being the Editor's secretary would have been more than enough to fulfil the ambitions of most secretaries, Lola was planning ahead. 'By this time, I had it in my mind to do a journalists' course and I had it in my mind also that this was going to be my last job as a secretary.'

And things turned out exactly as Lola predicted. The *London Daily News* never attained the circulation figures that its proprietor had hoped for. Underpriced at 10p and in deep financial difficulties, the fledgling newspaper closed one Friday in 1987: staff had one week to find alternative employment. But it's an ill wind that blows nobody any good; at least Lola got to go on her journalism course sooner than she expected.

What made her think she had it in her to succeed as a journalist?

I think the quality of an outstanding journalist is the ability not to give up. Even when you think, 'I'm not going to get this story right', don't give up. Always go back and keep going. I had to do it often as a secretary. When the going gets tough everyone gets hysterical. We all get hysterical. You just sit there until you get the stuff done. I would sit there if it took me till midnight to get whatever it was done. If anything needed doing, I didn't moan – I did it. And I have a very good memory, which probably helps as well.

A sense of humour is a great asset, too.

It helps when you can laugh in the face of adversity, like when the *London Daily News* went down. The Monday after it happened, I took my camera to work – I got this marvellous picture of Magnus with Peter Lynch, the News Editor. All the photos on that Monday were of smiling people . . . It had been such a good concern. We'd all had the chance to produce something that was worthwhile.

Lola's confidence didn't just come from her buoyant personality. Her temperament was ideally suited to her work environment and, equally important, she was given every encouragement by colleagues.

People have told me I *can* write, which is quite flattering. It's what you need . . . Journalists are my favourite type of people. I think they're very eccentric – like I am . . . and they've got strange habits – like I've got! The day before American Independence Day 1986 Neal Ascherson said to me, 'You'll be an editor one day.' And I have to take that at face value, because Neal isn't the sort of man who'd say something like that for some sort of joke. I shall always think of that.

So, don't be too surprised if Lola Hatmil makes it to the Guinness Book of Records by becoming Fleet Street's first black woman Editor. Lola already has her feet on the bottom rung of the editorial ladder, having passed her journalism course at the London College of Printing and having landed her first job as a reporter on a small trade newspaper. But does she see her days as a secretary as having been wasted? 'Not at all! I wouldn't have missed being a secretary for the past fifteen years for the world, because that proves that you can still start out as a journalist at thirty-two.'

The late starter

Does the difficulty a secretary experiences in moving up the career ladder always mean that she or he will always be a late starter?

Lola recognized that her years as a secretary were not wasted. It takes time to gain experience and contacts, and she will find both invaluable as her career develops.

But while a secretary may have an excellent understanding of the workplace and much practical experience, she may find herself overtaken by someone with the right paper qualifications – maybe even someone straight out of college.

Not everyone is academic, however, and exam results are not always an indication of how a person will perform in a job. Lola had an unpromising school career, but for her motivation was the key to success. She was happy in her job and therefore motivated and she saw her position as secretary as only a stage in a much broader career.

Planning a career

Planning a career requires a set of short-term and long-term aims. Although Lola didn't consciously think along these lines, it's clear from what she says that she spotted and took opportunities as they arose. In order to set yourself some career objectives, you must be able to look at your own strengths and weaknesses and compare them realistically with the qualities and skills needed in the job you wish to do. As well as self-appraisal, ask your boss and senior colleagues about the possibilities for career development in the organization you work for. Can you taken on extra responsibilities, for instance? What training do you need?

Lola made her ambitions very clear and was fortunate enough to have been advised and encouraged by a number of sympathetic colleagues. Although she was in the right place at the right time, Lola really made her own luck. So what *were* her short- and long-term aims?

Short-term

- to gain as much experience as possible of every aspect of journalism and newspaper production
  (she was helped in this by the secretarial training scheme then operated by *Times* Newspapers)
- to match her own talents and personal qualities with the available career opportunities
  (in this, Lola sought the advice of colleagues and won their respect by her ability to cope under stress and work to deadlines)
- to move as far up the secretarial ladder as possible
  (working for the Editor gave her an overview of the entire newsgathering and editorial function)
- to study for a professional qualification
  (it was not enough to be told she could write; a qualification proved it, and gave her the added self-respect and recognition enjoyed by the professionals with whom she worked)

Long-term

- to obtain employment as a junior reporter
- to acquire a reputation for spotting a newsworthy story that could be taken up by the national press
- to move into a senior editorial position with a small-circulation local or trade newspaper
- to move to a job on a national daily newspaper
- to become its editor!

We have speculated about Lola's long-term aims, but it seems reasonable to suppose that with faith in herself and the ability to back it up she will be able to achieve them.

Status and self-image

What are the skills essential in developing a successful and satisfying secretarial career?

- Communicating
- Problem-solving
- Decision-making
- Dealing with people
- Organizing time

- Allocating resources
- Planning meetings and visits
- Running an efficient office

At first glance these would seem to be a list of skills required of a senior manager. Yet this impressive portfolio of talents is no more than would be expected of any competent secretary.

Unfortunately we all know people who, when questioned about their occupation, say coyly: 'Oh, I'm only a secretary.' Why is it that the position of secretary is considered to carry less status and respect than other jobs which are equally skilled or demanding?

Look at a typical 'line and staff' organization chart for an average company. The post of secretary is shown as an adjunct to that of the manager for whom he or she works, and the status of the secretary is also determined by the status of the secretary's chief. Yet a secretary working for a junior manager may be just as able, well-qualified and experienced as his or her colleague who works for the Chief executive and gets paid twice as much.

June Tatum, President of the Executive Secretaries' Club, puts forward the view that when a secretary is 'running an office for the Chairman or Managing Director, we reckon she is managing anyway'. In other words, 'top secretaries should be managers in their own right'. The secretary-manager, after all, controls an office, staff and a budget. June Tatum continues:

> Once you're a top secretary for a Managing Director, you're dealing with budgets for all Departments. You've got to read the balance sheet, know about personnel, know about the production side if it's a manufacturing concern and deal with the workforce generally. And you're feeding information into your boss that he must know in order to determine what to do with his company. While you are involved with this, you are in fact running the office for him – the other directors helping, but you are more or less kingpin.

But just how often are secretaries recognized and rewarded for these management skills by being made a Director? Helen Hutty, Group Finance Director of Cecil MacDonald & Co Ltd (dealing in duty free wines and spirits and luxury goods), recalls her career as a secretary:

I went to secretarial college. After that, I left and went to work for a company in London and I was with them when I was between the ages of eighteen and twenty-three. Strangely enough, I worked for a woman in those days (the late 1950s) – it was practically unheard of. When I got married I moved to Camberley in Surrey and I went to work for the Town Planning Officer – local government. I was there for three years. I dealt with the public as well as being secretary. From there I went to work for Johnson's Wax. I was there until 1964 when I had my daughter. They gave me leave of absence and in those days that was very unusual because there wasn't any provision for maternity leave. I had three months off, which was six weeks before my daughter was born and then when she was six weeks old I had a nanny and went back to work. So again, that was really something. I wanted to work and I think that's got something to do with climbing the ladder, because women who have time off to have babies and then wait until the child is going to its first school or has reached the age of ten have to make one hell of an effort to get back into the swing of things.

Helen and her husband divorced in 1967 and she moved back to London to work as secretary to the Sales Director of a wines and spirits company.

He had twenty-six salesmen and really he taught me such a lot about the business we were in. But he also taught me quite a lot by default because he spent so much time out of the office that I found I was just naturally handling problems as they arose. He was very encouraging and he allowed me to make decisions. I think that had a lot to do with my development.

I don't think they [management] ever think of a secretary as being a manager. And yet she deals with everything, and she has an insight into the business.

After several years, we had a dynamic young man come into the company. He'd been to Harvard Business School and I can only imagine that he saw my potential and suggested that I move into the top job. I then worked for the Managing Director and I did the Chairman's private work – I looked after his stocks and shares. Then he had some properties and I looked after those. But you can only do as much as the man you're working for allows you to do, and this was a person who let me make decisions, sit in on meetings and put forward a viewpoint.

In October of that year there was a big boardroom upheaval and the man I was working for – the MD – was ousted by the non-executive directors. I was offered a position with the son of the Chairman whom I'd actually trained since he was eighteen, and I didn't feel it was on. I felt I knew more than this young man; all right, he was the son, but it just didn't feel right somehow. But he became the Managing Director. I'm not saying that I could have taken over the role of MD, but certainly I could do more than the young man who was coming in to do the job. If they'd had the foresight, they could have sent me away on a course and they could have trained me a little bit more.

Luckily, Helen had met the boss of another wines and spirits company when she'd organized an overseas trade delegation to Germany. She'd even been offered a job by the man and the offer was now renewed. Before the boardroom coup, Helen had been reluctant to move. Now she accepted graciously.

Mr Sankey, the Chairman and Managing Director of the company I now work for, invited me to take over the role of Company Secretary. Well, my forte was administration and a Company Secretary is really legal and finance, so I was a bit tentative about it. I was very impressed that he should have thought of me and I suppose it presented such a challenge. The lady who had the position was near to retiring, but she agreed to stay on for six more weeks and train me. I can only say that it was intense training, and that's something else you don't find very often – one woman helping another to that extent. I think they're often a bit frightened of their own positions. Well, that's what happened, and that was in 1975. Four years later I was made a Director.

Helen Hutty is now in her mid-fifties, having achieved her ambition to become a Director at the age of forty-five. She still has a few years to go before it is her turn to retire.

I think I've made it. I don't want the Managing Director's job. I think I'm quite happy and I would like to see out the rest of my working life in this job and retire at sixty. I'm not necessarily going to stop working, but I'd like to do something for myself. It might be something to do with interior decor – that's what I do as a hobby – or something to do with antiques. Hopefully, I shan't have to worry too much about making money in order to survive.

What qualities did Helen Hutty have that enabled her to succeed in the world of senior management?

- common sense: I think I can deal with people and I'm very organized;
- the ability to cope under pressure: I'm happier working under pressure;
- ambition: I was always wanting to be top dog;
- self-confidence: I think for someone to have faith in you you've got to have faith in yourself;
- being career-minded: The job changes I made when I was younger I made purposefully;
- willingness to learn: Each job I took, I took with a view to learning as much as I possibly could.

Knowledge is power

Helen's point about learning as much as she possibly could is echoed by many successful businessmen and women. Eleanor MacDonald, a management training consultant and a youthful seventy-seven-year-old veteran whose boardroom career has spanned two generations, believes the key to success is 'knowing how to question. Why am I doing this? Where does this job lead? From thinking and reflecting, we come up with judgement and we are paid for our judgement.'

June Tatum agrees. 'Top women are more dedicated. They will solve problems at the desk rather than go off on the golf course.' A secretary should 'learn everything she can about her own department and also about the departments around her. You're sitting at your desk. Now – do you know where the work is coming to you from? When you've finished a report, do you know where it is going to? Learn what your own job is worth.'

Why did Helen Hutty learn as much of what was going on around her as possible? 'Obviously, in order to do my job better. But also to know enough about the business interests of my company to be able to take independent decisions.'

And along with the privileged position of secretary to the Managing Director comes access to information which is denied to junior employees and even middle management. There's probably no better way of learning what a business is all about than becoming the chief's right hand and being involved in the decision-making process.

Inside knowledge is particularly useful in media industries where secretaries have traditionally moved into top creative jobs, having understood how the centres of power operate within their companies. Lynda MacDonnell is a Creative Director with Aspect Hill Holliday, a West-End advertising agency.

I wanted to be a barrister. I studied for a couple of years and then I thought it was all too boring. It would be too long before I earned any money. So I went and worked as a secretary for a travel agency in Park Lane. I worked for John Carter who wrote for the *Sunday Times* then (he does *The Holiday Programme* on BBC TV now) and we went on trips, and I wrote little bits which he rewrote.

I soon got bored and a friend told me 'advertising's really good fun, and there are some nice people'. So I went for a job at a firm called Dolly and Birnbach and it did seem like huge fun. I met a lot of people there whom I still keep in touch with – Peter Mead who is now Abbott Mead Vickers, Tony Brignall, Neal Godfrey, John Collins – all the people there now have their own agencies. It was a real ginger group and I was David Abbott's secretary for two years. I didn't really get any training because it was a very intimidating atmosphere, particularly for a young secretary. It was the sixties – affairs were rife in the agency and I was teased unmercifully. It would now be regarded as sexual harassment, but then it was just seen as having a good time.

Then I went to Byfield Mead, started up by Brian Byfield and Peter Mead. It was a tiny place. There was one other writer, and when he was off sick I had to do it. All the ads were discussed all the time. As a secretary in the Creative Department I heard a lot of criticism of people's ads inside and outside the agency. So you pick up a lot of useful tips such as you don't use words like 'unique'. How to write so it reads as if it's just a conversation –

that's the technique, I think, of copywriting. It changes, obviously, depending on whether you're writing about army officers or fish fingers. But whatever you're writing about it's got to be readable. People don't have to read what you've put down.

My break came when they wanted someone to work on the Milton Keynes Development Corporation account, writing their brochures and stuff like that. So I said, 'I'll do that'. Nobody else wanted the job because it involved going to Milton Keynes twice weekly – great excitement for me, but everybody else thought it would be a huge bore. It meant hanging around the Development Corporation offices and going with the architects to see the new housing developments. They had a series of seven-year plans – what they wanted to achieve: nice things like 'no building should be taller than the tallest tree'; it was a nice, advertisable idea.

When I was a secretary, I never thought to the future. I just thought, 'I'm bored being a secretary . . . what else can I do? I don't want to do this.' But of course, there was a lot of work involved in becoming a copywriter. I was up every night and working every weekend just to get a portfolio together while I was working as a secretary.

I invented fly-proof curtains, frozen soups and a plain water spray – this is before I knew about Evian spray – and I did a campaign for each of these products, press and television, you know, and posters for all my invented products. Well, I had a girl friend who wanted to be an art director, so we worked together.

After working on brochures and advertising for Milton Keynes, Lynda moved to another agency where her talents as a copywriter were quickly recognized.

My first major campaign I suppose was Mary Quant – it was the first time cosmetics had been advertised by poster. My ads read 'Mary's lipstick dipstick', 'Mary takes the plunge'. I'm also fond of the ads I wrote for Clarks shoes – 'Looks aren't everything, but try telling that to a woman', and there's a picture of two little girls and loads of Clarks shoes all over the shop and 'Even Clarks can be agony sometimes' with a little girl who can't choose between lots of different styles of shoes. That one won Best Ad of the Year. Another favourite of mine was for Barclays Bank: 'Hands up those that are paid in cash!' – and it's just a frightened man looking down the barrel of a big shotgun into a stocking-masked face. I'm thrilled to death seeing an ad appear in the paper that you love, that's come out of your agency.

Women at the top

When Lynda MacDonnell broke through into the male-dominated world of advertising copywriting she was very much an exception. It is even rarer for a woman to rise to the position of Director.

Two and a half years ago I was the only lady Creative Director in the advertising world. Now I can think of several. Nowadays, it isn't unusual to find women writers, art directors, production controllers and media planners, as well as being the heads of these departments. I don't think there's any particular feeling against women doing well. In fact, our Chairman is a lady but it's rare. She's probably the only lady Chairman in advertising.

But there are a lot of women who don't want to become managers or directors as it does involve quite a sacrifice. I've got a home and a husband but no kids – it would be quite difficult to fit them in.

On Monday night I worked late – I left here about half-past midnight – I was seeing a client. Tonight, I've got to go out on a pitch until about one o'clock. So this week I wouldn't be seeing my children, if I had any at all. I see my husband because he's still up then. Men have the same thing, except they're more used to it. It's more acceptable for a bloke to work late than a mother.

Women are, increasingly, finding their way into top jobs, competing on equal terms with men. But while a man can cope with managerial pressures because he has a secretary and a wife to support him at home, a woman in a similar job often has the added responsibilities of running a household and looking after children.

An essential part of being a secretary is to manage your boss's time and to prioritize tasks. Lynda sees this as very important in helping to take the stress off her: 'As a secretary, you have to be very calm in chaos. The best secretaries are quite bossy. They will ring you up and say, "You have to go to this meeting *now*", or "I know you've been in this meeting quite long enough: you've got to go and do this or your day is going to stack up." '

It's this aptitude for time management which enables many ex-secretaries to cope with the conflicting demands of running a business and a home.

Opportunities for secretaries

Since more and more women have moved into management, is it true to say that it has become easier for a younger generation of secretaries to follow them? The signs are that this is not the case. Lynda MacDonell admits:

> It's a real pain breaking in new secretaries so, selfishly, I'd rather they stayed in their job. You see, they always go through that period when they're no use to me at all. Because they don't want to be a secretary any more. They spend all their day writing copy, so they're not secretaries. On the other hand they're not copywriters either. Our Chairman, Jennifer Love, for instance, has a secretary who's been with her for seven years and knows everything about her life. If Jennifer fell under a bus, I think Jeanette could carry on without her for a while.

In spite of her own success, Lynda doesn't see being a secretary as conferring any advantages – in fact, quite the opposite:

> I wouldn't recommend being a secretary as a route now to copywriting. There are far too many people with a start on you really. I would say it's better to go through the traditional routes these days, like going through the London College of Printing, or doing a foundation course, or taking one of the DNAD's courses. In the sixties it was a little easier.

Making the first move

Some industries or areas of employment are more likely than others to promote or retrain secretaries for more senior or specialized posts. If you are hoping to use your position as a secretary as a stepping-stone to another career, then you might consider seeking employment in one of the following areas:

- personnel
- recruitment
- sales
- marketing
- PR
- journalism
- publishing
- computers

On the other hand, if you know from the outset that you want a job as, say, a copywriter or a personnel manager, there's a strong argument against becoming a secretary at all. The secretarial route to management is seldom an easy one, and there's no guarantee that once you get into secretarial work you will necessarily get out as and when you want to.

Our three ex-secretaries all displayed considerable confidence and ambition, backed up by sound skills and sheer talent. Unfortunately, the signs are that it's not getting any easier for secretaries to become high-flying managers because formal training and qualifications are so important to prospective employers. New developments in vocational training, under the auspices of the National Council for Vocational Qualifications, may help to raise the status of secretarial jobs and qualifications, and so give secretaries access to greater career development. Names and addresses of some organizations which can help and advise you about further training are given at the end of this book.

It must be said, however, that secretaries do still have certain advantages over those who are equipped only with paper qualifications:

- their experience of organizing and coping under stress will be seen as a valuable asset to any organization;
- they have the opportunity to observe at close quarters exactly what it's like to work in their chosen career;
- they can build up important contacts within an organization and become known and respected by senior management;
- they can observe over a long period how the centres of power operate within the organization, and familiarize themselves with the rules of 'office politics'.

61

The last of the above points should not be underestimated. New recruits to any organization always take time to find their feet, whereas the sure-footed ex-secretary who understands the way in which a certain manager likes to receive information, or his probable response to a given set of circumstances, will quickly lay the foundations of a lasting career.

The last word belongs to Eleanor MacDonald, a woman who, in more than fifty years in business, must have more experience of management than most men: 'Women must help other women. With the correct qualifications and expertise, you are going to establish positions of respect and you are going to make it possible for future generations of women to follow in your steps.'

5

Getting the Job you Want

It used to be accepted that secretarial work was a useful stopgap for the average girl between leaving school without any qualifications and becoming a housewife.

The same is hardly true today. Such is the shortage of competent secretaries, especially in London, that secretarial work has become the centre of a huge media 'hype'. All of a sudden it's respectable and even trendy for an intelligent school leaver to choose secretarial work not as a stopgap, but as a career.

The tempting prospect of earning anything up to £30,000 a year as a top-flight PA must have lured many a bright-eyed eighteen-year-old away from a career in teaching or nursing. It would be wrong to suggest that all the old prejudices have been swept away, since in many quarters the job of secretary is still regarded as 'subservient' and 'women's work'. Nevertheless, for £30,000 a year there are an awful lot of people who wouldn't mind being 'number two'!

Secretarial work and the concept of success are no longer incompatible: many people find ample room for personal development, responsibility and achievement without ever having to leave the profession. Others decide to move on: but few ever regret the experience and skills gained from a career in secretarial work.

Taking stock of the situation

Very few people can remain happily in the same job for the whole of their working lives. Fortunately, the world of work today is constantly changing and creating many new opportunities for switches of job or even career.

In chapter four we met three people who had used their secretarial experience to get out of secretarial work and into other careers. Not everyone wants to do anything quite so radical; but secretaries do have many transferable skills which make them potentially very attractive to a wide range of employers. Unfortunately, not all employers are aware of the range of competences which secretaries can offer, and it's often up to the individual secretary to 'market' him or herself in order to get the right job.

The first question to ask yourself is: 'Am I happy in my present job?' If the answer in an unqualified yes, then perhaps you should resist the temptation to change your job just because everyone thinks it is a good idea to do so every five years or so.

Society today is founded upon an idea of success through hierarchical status and salary. But it's important to remember that success doesn't mean the same thing to everybody. Job satisfaction is a rare and valuable quality and (assuming your 'happiness' is not really laziness!) there's nothing wrong with staying in a job for as long as it continues to provide whatever you want from it.

If you cannot honestly say that you are happy with your present job, then there are a host of other questions you will need to ask yourself:

- *What do I like and dislike about my present job?* Understanding this will help you make the right choices when you look for a new job.
- *Would I prefer more, or less, responsibility?* People tend to assume that getting a 'better' job means getting one which carries greater responsibility. This is by no means universally true. Many people prefer to be responsible only for their own work – not for that of others – and this is nothing to be ashamed of!
- *Which of my previous jobs did I like most and least? Why?*
- *How important to me are the people I work with? Would I prefer to work alone or in a group? Would I rather work for myself?*
- *Would I mind travelling or relocating?*
- *How important is money to me?*
- *Would I be prepared to retrain? If so, do I have the resources to support myself during training?*
- *Do I want to stay in secretarial work? Why?*
- *Could secretarial work provide a 'back door' to a new profession?*
- *Do I have any specific alternative jobs in mind?*

Once you have answered these questions you should be in a better position to understand what you want or don't want from a job. The next important step is to try and decide if you match up to what an employer wants from you.

Taking stock of yourself

It is all very well coming up with a long list of job demands: but don't expect them to be met if they are unrealistic. Age is one factor which cannot be ignored, as Liz Hodgkinson points out in her *Working Woman's Guide*:

> A word . . . about being a secretary: if you are in your mid- to late twenties, it really is time to start thinking about doing something else. After the age of thirty-five, when executives start to find their professional feet, a secretary can discover her days are numbered. A quick look at ads for secretaries reveals that few are wanted after age thirty-five. That is also when salary levels are at their highest: after this age, they tend to go down again, and your employability diminishes. Few people – men at least – like a middle-aged secretary.

The best that anyone can do is to set targets which are attainable within the bounds of one's own limitations. But in order to do this, it's necessary to think very carefully and produce a list of personal skills, strengths and weaknesses.

As a secretary, which skills spring immediately to mind? Shorthand? Typing? WP? These are the bread and butter skills which you have to have just to get a secretarial job; but they are not necessarily the skills which turn a good secretary into an excellent one.

If you note down every task – however small – which you undertake during a typical working day, you will realize just how wide-ranging secretarial work is. You should be able to define the skills you need to have in order to carry out each task; for example, using the telephone efficiently demands good communication skills. Your final list will probably look something like this:

- *Mechanical skills*: shorthand, keyboarding etc. Essential for a secretary, and useful in other areas of work (e.g. journalism, management);
- *Problem-solving*: the essence of any secretarial job;
- *Handling information;*
- *Dealing with people* (human resource management);
- *Working with figures* (e.g. book-keeping, accounting, preparation of statistical data);
- *Making decisions;*

- *Giving direction* (especially if you control other staff);
- *Co-ordinating things, people and events*: e.g. the careful attention to timing which is essential when organizing a large meeting or conference;
- *Communicating*: verbally, in writing, graphically and non-verbally (through self-presentation);
- *Public relations*: tact, diplomacy, persuasiveness, creativity, self-control;
- *Creative skills*: e.g. form design, production of material using desktop publishing skills;
- *Familiarity with new technology*.

There are of course problems with this type of list. First, it doesn't include any indication of your qualifications to do a particular job. For example; supposing you want to use your secretarial experience to get into management. You may use management skills such as decision-making and problem-solving every day, but if you don't have a management qualification you'll have to persuade a potential employer that you are management material. Self-marketing can be very important.

Second, your list of skills may include a host of skills which you use every day but absolutely detest having to use. You may have to undertake book-keeping duties or take charge of the payroll for dozens of employees, but if you hate figure work and never want to have anything to do with it again, this is one skill which you might not wish to promote! On the other hand, you could always try emphasizing the responsibility involved rather than the degree of mechanical skill.

The other problem is the fact that a skills list includes those skills which you aren't very good at, as well as those in which you excel. That's why it's so important to analyse your personal strengths and weaknesses. It can be very difficult to be objective about one's own good points and bad points. Anyone who has to undergo regular job appraisals will know how awful it is to have weaknesses and errors of judgement pointed out and talked about in embarrassing detail. Nevertheless, someone else's point of view can be very valuable. If you don't feel you can make an ally of your boss, why not ask a close friend whose opinions you respect? Together, you should be able to construct a pretty accurate picture of what you have to offer an employer.

Taking advice

So – you now know what you do each day, and how good you are at doing it. You've probably also got some ideas about what you would like to do next, whether this involves moving to another secretarial job or trying to start out in a completely new career. But are your ideas and ambitions realistic? It could be time to take advice.

- *Career analysis*: Professional careers analysts offer a variety of services including computer analysis, aptitude testing, counselling and personality profiling. The objective is to help clients decide which careers are most suitable for them – but fees are very high and results carry no guarantee. Nor is any assistance offered with the soul-destroying business of actually getting a job.
- *College careers service*: Usually free to students and former students. Advice will also be available to intending students about any retraining courses currently on offer.
- *Job Centres*: Not generally very good for secretarial work, but can advise on retraining and self-employment schemes.
- *Business development agencies*: Local organizations which offer advice on setting up small businesses.
- *Libraries*: Should have a good selection of useful reference books on careers and training courses. Will also have directories which you can use to find out the names and addresses of potential employers.
- *Professional bodies*: e.g. Law Society, Institute of Agricultural Secretaries. Can provide information about entry to different professions.
- *Employment agencies*: Are mainly interested in getting you signed on their books, but smaller, friendlier agencies will sometimes take the time to advise you if they don't have the right kind of work for you. Agencies deal in permanent, as well as temporary, work and can be very useful in getting you interviews for secretarial jobs. They can also provide extra training (e.g. in WP or interview skills) if they want you to temp for them – but this facility is entirely at their discretion. Be prepared to undergo lots and lots of irksome tests in everything from shorthand to spelling; they won't accept your word (or your certificates) at face value!

The right strategy to get the right job

Making the most of your boss

Not all managers are sympathetic to their secretaries' career aspirations. To quote Wendy Syer, PA to Sir Campbell Adamson: 'Bosses seem to think it's a slight if you want to progress.' Having developed a good working relationship with a secretary over a period of months or years, it's understandable that a manager might want to discourage his secretary from leaving.

On the other hand, there are many managers who recognize the potential of their secretaries and seek to develop it. If your boss is sympathetic to your aims, he or she can make an excellent ally. But what exactly can a good boss do for your career? He or she can:

– offer advice on any extra training or qualifications which you will need to enter your chosen area of work;
– give support to any application for day release or subsidized evening class studies;
– indicate a willingness to help you put yourself forward for any suitable vacancies which arise within the organization;
– volunteer to give you a particularly good reference if and when you decide to apply for posts in other organizations;
– use the 'boss network' to make it known that you are looking for a new job.

But perhaps the most important and useful thing which your boss can do for you is just to be supportive and encouraging; to have one's aspirations received with sarcasm or hostility can be soul-destroying.

Using the Personnel Department

If you decide that there may be a place for you within your present organization, it's almost certainly worth arranging an informal discussion with a member of the Personnel Department. Make sure that the interview is with a senior member of staff, who can make authoritative statements about the type of opportunities and the time-scale which might be involved in obtaining the post you want.

At the very least, you should be able to determine whether or not you have a chance of achieving your ambitions without having to change firms. If the Personnel Officer is encouraging, and undertakes to consider you when suitable vacancies arise, set yourself a time-limit for achieving your goals. If, when that period has expired, you've applied for several suitable posts but not had a single interview, you'll probably have to look elsewhere.

Contacts and coincidences

Secretaries, like bosses, build up their own 'networks' over a period of time: contacts in other organizations and other secretaries who belong to the same professional organizations.

These informal contacts should not be underestimated, because many of the top secretarial posts are never seen in the 'Sits Vac' pages of local (or even national) newspapers. Many a post has been filled by personal recommendation, and by someone being in the right place at the right time.

Chance plays an important part in many career moves, particularly in the more 'unusual' secretarial posts. Liz Aydon, secretary to Richard Adams, was working as a legal executive in a firm of solicitors when her future employer walked in one day looking for someone to type an important letter. At that time she had no thoughts of returning to secretarial work:

> Mr Adams didn't have a secretary at the time, and there was a lot of fan mail building up in the background. At that stage I hadn't thought of leaving the Law, but I was very happy to come round on a Saturday morning and wade through some of the stuff. This went on for quite a while. My husband at the time was unemployed so the money was very helpful. Then Mr Adams asked me whether I'd like to work full-time for him and I had to think it through because although I wasn't happy in the Law, I hadn't thought of leaving. I realized after prayer that this was the right thing for me, and accepted. I've never regretted it, either.

'Celebrity' secretaries are not the only ones who may have come by their ideal jobs almost by accident. Alison works in a merchant bank in the City of London. She says:

> I was really getting fed up one day, and I sat down in the office

with a friend and had a very loud moan about the fact that I was wasting my life. This woman heard me moan, took me upstairs and offered me a new job in another department as a clerical officer.

Although the job was technically lower in status than that of a secretary, Alison was told that it would lead to promotion: and she has certainly found that it offered more scope for decision-making. 'Instead of getting a piece of paper and being told "type this", I get a problem to solve. If I still spend some time typing and filing, it's because it's essential to doing my job efficiently.'

Temps, too, often find that employers view them as potential members of the permanent staff, sometimes even tailoring a job to fit them. Rory Henneker, a male secretary, comments:

I was working as a temp in a certain company and my boss came up to me [this usually happens] and he asked me the usual questions: 'What are you doing? Why are you doing this? How did you learn these skills?' And I said, 'I was made redundant from a job as an Accounts Assistant'. He said: 'I have a vacancy for you – we'll incorporate your secretarial skills into the role.' As I didn't want to go back into Accounts, I declined his offer – but a similar thing could happen with a job I might be interested in.

Getting extra training

If you discover that you need extra training or qualifications in order to get your ideal job, you will need to incorporate a suitable training programme into your overall strategy. Some possible sources of training and work experience are listed below (there's also a list of useful addresses at the end of this book):

Training opportunities:	– on-the-job (in-house) (requires employer's support);
	– day release (requires employer's support);
	– evening classes;
	– private tuition (can be expensive);
	– correspondence course (expensive and not always reliable);

– private training by specialist firm or by employment agency (most agencies only train people who are going to work for them as temps);
– full-time course (you'll need a grant, or enough money to support yourself for the duration of the course, unless studying under the '21-hour' rule);

Work experience:
– your best bet could be an agency. Temping pays extremely well if you are anything like competent;
– you could also spend part of your holidays working in the sort of organization you'd like to be employed by. If you do well, you'll gain contacts, a good reputation and possibly referees. You might even be offered a job!

Researching the job market

As we have seen, many jobs are not won simply by replying to an advertisement in the local paper or Job Centre. On the other hand, it's no use sitting around and waiting for chance to land the right job in your lap, either. Careful research and canvassing can produce encouraging results.

If you look through a selection of old newspapers (local and national) you should be able to determine how often the right type of vacancy occurs, and the qualities and qualifications which are most frequently asked for by employers. You will also find out the names of potential employers, and possibly named individuals to write to within each organization. Libraries also have copies of business directories, 'Yellow Pages' etc., which can supply useful names and addresses.

By using all this information you can draft speculative letters, directed at specific people, emphasizing those points about yourself which you feel are most in demand for the job you want. Obviously it's no use lying about yourself; if advertisements consistently ask for someone with numerical ability and you can't add two and two, it would be pointless to make yourself out to be a born accountant. Clearly you would be applying for a job which you couldn't do – and this is why it's important to understand your own skills, strengths and weaknesses.

Marketing yourself

Everyone hates filling in application forms: why is there never enough space for the things you want to say, and too much space for the things you'd rather not go into at all? And what do they really want you to say in that terrible empty space marked 'any other information in support of your application'?

It's daunting. And yet a well-written letter and a beautifully-presented CV can work wonders for your career prospects, while a badly filled in form or a ten-page covering letter in illegible green biro will bring you down at the first fence.

No secretary should be incapable of good written presentation; this is, after all, one of the most important aspects of a secretary's job. But secretaries do still forfeit job opportunities simply through not taking time to think what an employer wants to read.

The Curriculum Vitae

Sandra Gibbons of Drake Personnel advises:

> A few years ago nobody had even heard of CVs, but now they've become really important. The girls who impress us the most are those who come in with their CVs typed up, spelt correctly and well laid out. What a prospective employer is looking for is detailed knowledge of exactly what you did in your previous positions. (*Ms London*, 5 April 1988)

A major point to remember with CVs is that they should be concise: one page if possible, and certainly no longer than two. The essential information to include is:

- *Personal details*: name, age, date of birth, address, telephone number;
- *Education*: schools, colleges, universities – with dates;
- *Qualifications*: in chronological order, with results;
- *Work experience*: every job (including holiday jobs if you haven't had much work experience) at least over the last ten years, in chronological or reverse chronological order. Give details of

your duties and responsibilities and (if room) the skills you
needed to carry out your duties;

- *Hobbies/leisure interests*: not crucial, but helps create an impression of your life and achievements outside work. Voluntary work
and awards such as the Duke of Edinburgh Gold Award could be
included here;
- *Referees*: names and addresses of two or three people who you
know are prepared to give you a good reference (this means you
have already asked them and they have said yes!). One should be
connected with your present job.

Remember to avoid gimmicks. Pink scented paper will not impress!
If you have researched your job and know your own strengths, the
facts should speak for themselves.

Speculative letters

A speculative letter is really a letter to a firm asking them to give you
a job, even though they aren't advertising any vacancies at the
moment. In order to stand any chance of getting even as far as an
informal interview, your letter has to be better than all the other
letters they get every week. It has to make a potential employer
think: 'This person has initiative and is obviously highly motivated.
This person sounds so good that I'd be mad not to offer him/her an
interview.'

Your letter will accompany your CV so there's no need for it to be
any longer than a single side. It should supply information which
isn't contained in the CV – such as your reasons for wanting to work
for the company, how your experience fits in with the company's
business, and why you believe they should consider employing you.

A word of warning: no matter how good they are, most of your
speculative letters will end in rejection. Don't be discouraged: one
positive response is enough!

Application forms

Everybody hates application forms, and with good reason. Many of
them are badly designed and don't ask the right questions, so many
people feel they are at a disadvantage from the start. In fact, quite a
few employers now invite applications by CV and covering letter.

If you do have to fill in one of the dreaded forms, remember:

- if you're not sure about how to fill it in, take a photocopy and practise on that before filling in the original;
- type if you're applying for a secretarial post – it's a way of showing what you can do. If you must write, use black ink and take great pains to be neat;
- try to think of something intelligent to put in the 'any other information' section, e.g. why you want the job, why you think you are an ideal candidate, the important aspects of your past experience, etc.;
- don't leave gaps: if you were unemployed for a time, say so. Gaps will only leave people wondering.

Surviving the interview

If there's one thing most people hate even more than an application form, it's an interview. Mouths go dry, knees tremble, minds go blank – and yet interviews are a two-way process, not an interrogation. The interviewing panel aren't there simply to ask difficult questions and delight in catching the interviewee off guard (though one does sometimes get that feeling with an unskilled interviewer!).

An interview gives you, the applicant, a chance to take a good look at your prospective employer and decide whether you like him or not. If you're offered the job you don't have to take it, any more than the company is obliged to offer it to you.

But inevitably, the majority of people dislike interviews because they feel they don't perform well. Secretaries really have no excuse for this nervousness, since they deal with difficult people and situations every day. Anyone who can pacify irate foreign business-men and deal diplomatically with corporate wives is capable of coping with a few interview questions.

According to Mary Spillane, an international 'colour consultant': 'When you meet someone for the first time it can be shown that as much as 60% of the impression you make is through the way you look, 20% through the way you act and only 20% through what you actually say' (*Drake Club*, April 1988). Looking smart is certainly an important part of any interview, but there's always a danger of going too far. Being well-presented is not the same as looking like a Christmas cake.

Other factors are equally important. The article in *Ms London* (5 April 1988) identified a number of interesting points, all gleaned from employment agencies. Potential perfect secretaries should have 'a happy disposition', should look 'confident and capable', should be 'objective' and should 'smile and be receptive'.

Moving on

If you're a highly skilled and experienced secretary with a good personality and appearance, then the world is your oyster, provided you are not over thirty-five! The fall in the number of young people in the 1990s should force employers to consider recruiting older secretaries as well as men, but at the moment secretarial work is a young woman's job.

Those secretaries who decide to move on and try to make a career in some other area of work may have problems. There's still a certain amount of prejudice against ex-secretaries; a feeling that if they had any talent they would have gone in for a 'proper' career in the first place.

But there are good signs, nevertheless. New technology and a more flexible attitude to work have begun to blur the line dividing secretarial work from other careers; 'managers' operate desktop VDUs and 'secretaries' carry out management tasks. Senior secretaries, personal assistants, management assistants . . . the distinctions are less obvious every day. Let's hope that this will make for greater opportunities for those with secretarial skills to put them to good use, without being made to feel ashamed of being secretaries.

6

We've Heard it all Before

The secretarial image: Take a letter, Myth Jones

'When people look at you, they see me' (Lionel Bainbridge to his secretary Sandra in the BBC comedy, *Brush Strokes*).

When people look at secretaries is that really all they see: an extension of the boss's image? It might be more honest to say that they see even less. Whether she's a nymphomaniac or a crabby old harridan, the secretary who adorns the pages of the *Sunday Sport* or features in a television sitcom is a gross distortion, an object of ridicule.

Take a look at the cartoons page of any tabloid newspaper or popular magazine and you'll almost certainly find at least one 'secretary' cartoon. We use the term 'secretary' loosely, because the interpretation placed upon it by cartoonists includes a large bust, long fingernails, mini-skirt and typewriter! So well established is the cliché that artists need only include one of these characteristics and the public knows instantly that the joke is about a secretary.

The cartoons reproduced in this chapter were taken from national newspapers and well-known magazines. You may find them offensive, but they are representative of the way secretaries are depicted and are by no means the worst examples!

Taken as a whole, there seem to be two main types of secretary as presented by the media. On the one hand we have the 'blonde bombshell' without a brain cell to her name and with a personality entirely subordinate to her pneumatic body. Her bosses are invariably male, middle-aged and exceedingly sexist. Her main characteristics are:

- incompetence ('all she's good at is being a perfect 36-24-36');
- 'dolly-bird' appearance;
- lack of intelligence;
- easy virtue;
- obsession with trivia (filing her nails, reading magazines etc);
- subservience;

The other type is the 'capable' secretary. This type is often presented as a frigid old spinster, physically unattractive and rather forbidding. Men perceive her as a threat, which they sometimes try to defuse with sarcasm, or as a mother-figure who will sort things out while they have a good old panic and retreat to the safety of their offices. Her main characteristics are:

- dowdiness (or at least lack of obvious glamour);
- common sense;
- dominance;
- intelligence;
- high moral standards;
- competence;
- (sometimes) sense of humour.

It would, of course, be foolish to imply that all media portrayals of secretaries fall neatly into one of these two categories. There are many exceptions. For example, secretaries in Mills and Boon romances are always physically attractive *and* competent. They may even appear dominant for a time, defying authority to protect their own interests. But in the end, they invariably fall victim to the often forceful charms of their big macho boss, and to hell with the secretarial career!

Examining media portrayals of secretaries in terms of cliché and category is a useful exercise, if only to illustrate some of the following points:

- generalization is rife;
- there's little understanding of what secretaries actually do (for 'secretary' read 'typist');
- media people clearly believe that secretaries and sex are inextricably linked;
- there is a widespread belief that secretarial work is for the terminally stupid girl who wants to have an affair with her big, strong, masculine boss. Any competent secretary who does not make eyes at her chief must be frigid and/or middle-aged;
- the media cannot cope with the idea of male secretaries (or female bosses);
- all male secretaries must be homosexual;
- any competent woman who is attractive and has a professional

77

attitude can't be a secretary, so she must be a Personal Assistant;
- the view persists that it isn't possible for a woman to combine a high-flying secretarial career with a normal family life.

Secs and sexism

Above all else, there's something in the role of the secretary which the public mind finds sexy and fascinating. Probably it has a great deal to do with the traditional male boss/female secretary scenario, and the persistent myth that a man and a woman can't work together without their hormones getting the better of them.

In this age of female executives and male PAs it would be nice to think that this cliché was on the way out, but far from it. In 1987, BBC1 broadcast a drama serial about an advertising agency called *Campaign*. Advertising itself has a rather raunchy image, and the combination of advertising and secretaries evidently proved too much for the writer, Gerard MacDonald.

One of the secretaries in the serial, Sally, has an affair with the agency's Director (David) and becomes pregnant. The following extract of dialogue illustrates vividly David's attitude to his mistress:

> (David) lowered his face back into Sally's hair.
> 'Phone,' he whispered.
> Either Sally was awake, or she came to consciousness quickly.
> 'Do you think –' she asked '– do you think I'm in New York to be your secretary?'
> David leaned over her naked back and grabbed the telephone cord.
> 'Of course not,' he said. With one hand he pulled the phone closer along the bedside table; he cupped the other around Sally's breast. 'You came as my plaything.'

Sally's boss, Sarah Copeland, has a no less humiliating opinion of her secretary:

> From the far side of the room Sarah weighed up her secretary's advantages. Sally was young. She had a delectable body, wonderful dark eyes, a luxuriant cloud of hair. On the other

hand, she was naïve, she read nothing but women's magazines, and she had no political skills. Outside the bedroom, any intelligent man would get tired of her within weeks. Or so Sarah had always assumed.

The other main secretarial character is Carol, who is described as 'the agency's oddity' because she does not conform to the accepted stereotype of an advertising agency secretary:

> For a start, she had a distinctly downmarket accent, originating somewhere in south-east London. Then there was her appearance. Where the rest of the agency secretaries tended to slim elegance, Carol had an exuberant body, constantly in conflict with the tight shirts and skirts she always wore (. . .). In Gordon's eyes, though, Carol had one quality which outweighed all the others. This was loyalty. . . . He had resisted several attempts to replace his secretary with a more presentable 'personal assistant'.

The idea of a 'personal assistant' as a sort of higher being in the secretarial world is borne out by the character of Alessandra, who is PA to the agency's managing director. She is 'an exceptionally beautiful blonde' with a manner which is described by her enemies as 'deep-frozen'. She is shown as a powerful figure, privy to many business and personal secrets, and tailored to fit the up-market world of the agency boardroom – quite a stark contrast to poor old Carol and sex-object Sally. Even the author's description of Carol's office has a patronizing quality:

> Carol had made a distinctive space for herself, filling it with a miniature jungle of plants, among the foliage of which stood small replicas of Snoopy and Woodstock, and framed photos of Carol's parents, taken at the seaside.

So there they are: three very different office stereotypes, but linked by a common bond: sex.

The power principle

One of the most durable clichés in literature and the media is the belief that secretaries and sex are inseparable.

Alessandra from *Campaign* is one side of the coin: the ice-cool blonde who calls the tune in her relationship. Much more typical is the secretary-victim: the eternal underling who seems to derive a curious, almost masochistic, pleasure from submitting to sexual domination.

In one typical story published by a popular women's magazine the heroine, Kara Fletcher, is attracted, against her will, to her fearsomely masculine boss, aptly-named Gavin Masters. Kara meets Gavin when she attends a business conference with her father. She finds him a wonderful and compelling figure; not only is he young, tall and strikingly handsome, he has already reached the dizzy heights of Company Chairman. Needless to say, she is quite unable to resist his blatantly sexist approach to recruitment:

'I'm looking for a good personal assistant, and I was hoping to poach you from your father.'

Kara stared at him. That was almost honest. 'And if you hadn't been able to poach me?'

'I'd have made you fall in love with me and you would have come anyway.'

Once in his employment, any thoughts Kara might have had about a strictly professional relationship quickly disappear. His idea of a secretary is evidently something between a galley slave and a concubine; and Kara's feeble attempts to assert herself are to no avail:

Now, as she knocked on Gavin Masters' door, she wondered if he would give any indication at all of the previous day's intimacies. She needn't have worried; he was as briskly efficient and impersonal as he had been the previous week.

'So, I'd be grateful if you'd let me know the number tomorrow night, and then you can get on with organizing some advertising for the gardener's cottage – in your own time, of course.'

'I see.' So he was going to start organizing her evenings, was he? 'Surely this is a PA's job?'

'So?'

'So I'll do it in working hours.'

'Are you daring to argue with me, Miss Fletcher?'

'Well –' She was bewildered. 'I suppose so – yes.'

'Then take my advice – don't.'

And it gets worse:

> Determined not to be beaten, Kara turned her cheek, fielding
> the kiss neatly, and grabbed for the door handle. Before she even
> touched it she was taken by a pair of vice-like hands and drawn
> back, like the fly into the spider's web.

Most professional secretaries would have handed in their notice –
and rightly so – at the first sign of impropriety. But Kara has clearly
never heard of feminism, and the moral of the story appears to be
that the ultimate fulfilment for a woman lies in marriage to a
powerful man. In this office fairy tale, Kara succeeds in reforming
her wayward boss through the magic of love; and by the end of the
story she has submitted willingly to his powerful passion:

> The touch of those lips, warm and firm and demanding on hers,
> unlocked the floodgates, behind which love and longing had
> gathered (. . .). As her lips moulded themselves to his, her hands
> stroked his neck, his hair, his strong, powerful shoulders (. . .).
> She wanted to give herself totally to him. (*Kara's Story*, in
> *Women's Weekly* 'Images of Love' series, 1984)

More than one real-life secretary has confessed to the feeling of
excitement which comes from an association with power. The
power-sex-hero worship matrix has been dealt with in many
permutations by the press, by films and books, almost always with
the secretary in a subordinate role. Often, like Perry Mason's Della
Street, or James Bond's Moneypenny, she's depicted as a surrogate
wife or mother, content to protect her boss from the outside world,
happy to do all the work and take none of the credit.

Miss Moneypenny, created by Ian Fleming in the 1950s, is a
deskbound figure who leads an unglamorous existence in stark
contrast to the danger and excitement which are part of James
Bond's daily life. There is a certain unspoken sexual dynamism
between Bond and Moneypenny, which surfaces only as light
banter. As this extract shows, Moneypenny always shows concern
for Bond's welfare:

Miss Moneypenny screwed up her nose. 'But James, do you really drink and smoke as much as that? It can't be good for you, you know.' She looked up at him with motherly eyes.

But 007 puts her firmly in her place:

'Now don't you start on me, Penny.' Bond walked angrily towards the the door. He turned round. 'Any more ticking off from you and when I get out of this place I'll give you such a spanking you'll have to do your typing off a block of Dunlopillo.'

We can only imagine Moneypenny's response. Presumably she simply smiled coyly and got on with her typing. Today, she would be more likely to report Bond for sexual harassment.

Writers often present the secretary as a contrast to a powerful and dynamic hero. What they don't seem willing to do is to present secretaries as powerful figures in their own right, either at work or in their private lives. More often than not they are also seen as submissive partners in sexual relationships. This vision of the secretary is particularly damaging to the women – and men – who are now making their mark as today's top-flight secretaries and PAs.

A figure of fun?

A boss advertised for a new secretary, but was uncertain about his ability to choose the best person for the job – so he hired a very expensive recruitment consultant to advise him.

When the two men had finished interviewing the applicant, the consultant summed up their qualifications for the job: 'Now, the first young lady – she had a great deal of relevant experience; the second displayed maturity and good judgement; and the third had extremely fast shorthand and typing speeds. It's a difficult choice to make – but have you come to a decision?'

'Yes,' replied the boss. 'I'll have the one in the red mini-skirt.'

A joke? Maybe. But there's more than a grain of truth in it. How often have you felt that you lost a job because one of the other candidates had longer legs or a more shapely bottom? There are so many clichés surrounding the secretary in popular mythology that she has become almost a figure of fun: a caricature of reality.

Anthony Burton, writing in *A Programmed Guide to Office Warfare* (Secker and Warburg 1969), gives the following semi-serious advice to managers:

> There are many, many advantages to having a competent secretary . . . (but) if the choice lies between maximum competence and ugliness, and minimum competence and beauty, the selection must go to the latter (. . .).
> First, it will make your life more pleasant. Secondly, she will excite the envy of your colleagues. Thirdly, she will do wonders for the morale of the department. Fourthly, she can be deployed so as to disarm the opposition. To enlarge on the final point: suppose you have a favour to ask of another department, you send your beautiful secretary, for who could refuse such charm? If you have bad news to impart, again you send the ravishing beauty to calm the savage beast.

The assumption appears to be that the secretary is simply an extension of the male ego or a symbol of power, just like a mahogany desk or a revolving leather armchair.

But secretaries are not part of the office furniture: they have minds and feelings of their own – a fact rarely acknowledged by humorists. Michael Green, in his *Art of Coarse Office Life* (Century Hutchinson 1987), attempts to look inside the mind of a secretary and translates her imagined priorities and preoccupations into the humorous 'organization chart reproduced on p.84. According to Michael Green:

> The secretary's power scheme is chaotic because she has two loyalties, one to her boss and the other to her private life, and there is a constant battle between the two (. . .). Those sections of the office power structure which affect daily life are the secretary's priority, chiefly the switchboard, the telex room, the post room and the maintenance man. Someone who can mend her desk lamp or fix the typewriter is obviously more important than the chairman or managing director.

Although there's a grain of truth in what he says, Green's picture of the secretarial mentality homes in on two elements which will not please professional secretaries: sex and trivia. The secretary's life

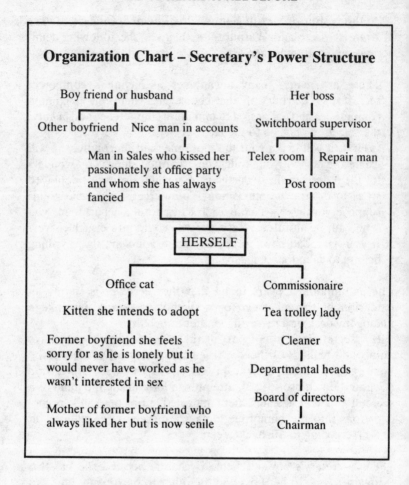

Organization Chart – Secretary's Power Structure

Boy friend or husband

Other boyfriend — Nice man in accounts

Man in Sales who kissed her passionately at office party and whom she has always fancied

Her boss

Switchboard supervisor

Telex room — Repair man

Post room

HERSELF

Office cat

Kitten she intends to adopt

Former boyfriend she feels sorry for as he is lonely but it would never have worked as he wasn't interested in sex

Mother of former boyfriend who always liked her but is now senile

Commissionaire

Tea trolley lady

Cleaner

Departmental heads

Board of directors

Chairman

appears to revolve around subjugation to one of two men – her boyfriend/husband and her boss. What of her other preoccupations? Former boyfriends, men she has flirted with, cats, kittens and old ladies – hardly the image of the sleek, self-assured professional.

On the other hand, Michael Green does concede that the soft-hearted but rather stupid secretary has at least one rival – the Dragon:

Perhaps the most important power source in any office is the chief executive's secretary (. . .). Never quarrel with them. They guard the portals of power and nobody passes in without their permission. If you wish to be a failure in life, offend the chief executive's secretary.

In office humour, secretaries seldom have the last word. Secretaries are generally seen as young and brainless:

- 'I don't do carbon copies – they only repeat the mistakes!'
- 'Her qualifications? No "O" levels, no "A" levels, and no knickers!'
- 'All she's good at is being a perfect 36-24-38!'

In many cartoon situations, men behave in the same appalling way towards their secretaries as they do towards their wives. In the captions below, the word 'secretary' could easily be replaced by the word 'wife':

- 'How about a secretary-swapping afternoon?'
- 'Yes, I am an advocate of free competition, but not with my secretary.'

Feminism is often the butt of humour and the secretary is the archetypal anti-feminist stereotype. In these cartoon captions, secretaries are seen to provoke sexual harassment by their mere presence, bringing out the beast in the most unlikely of men:

- (Balding, bespectacled and apologetic boss to embarrassed secretary) 'I'm afraid I must replace you, Miss Thomas – you are releasing in me frustrations and passions which I normally reserve for the business.'
- (Hopeful, middle-aged boss to surprised secretary) 'I was wondering Miss Prossier, if you have ever given any consideration to the idea of making a complete fool of me . . . ?'

Conversely, women who stand up for themselves, or who hold positions of power, are mocked as abnormal and unattractive, presumably because they pose a threat to male dominance. It is these women who interpret any chance remark – if made by a man – as sexual harassment:

- (Bewildered boss to fierce, crop-haired secretary) 'Sexual harassment? Because I admired your notebook?'

"Sorry J. B., there's been a takeover bid."

"I'm afraid I must replace you, Miss Thomas—you are releasing in me frustrations and passions which I normally reserve for the business."

"I was wondering, Miss Prossier, if you have ever given any consideration to the idea of making a complete fool of me . . .?"

HOTEL

"I'm sorry, Fiona, but it's the only way I can tell you how I feel . . ."

These cartoons are reproduced by kind permission of *Punch*.

- (Frumpish college principal to buxom blonde student) 'On leaving you'll have all the necessary office skills: shorthand, typing, filing, self-defence . . .'

The office party is a perennial source of secretarial humour of the worst kind:

- (Jocular sales manager dictating shorthand to enraged blonde secretary in mini-skirt) 'P.S. See you at the firm's Christmas party – our secretaries are always good for a bit of fun!'
- (Ugly secretary to manager at party) 'Do you want to pull a cracker?' (Manager) 'Yes. Go away!'

One fact which emerges from all the examples of secretarial humour which we have studied is the total lack of understanding between men and female secretaries. It appears to us that, because of this communication barrier, men are rather afraid of their secretaries and feel that they have to diminish the threat by mocking and belittling them.

One of the saddest, and yet the funniest, cartoons that we have found illustrates the communication problem very well indeed. It shows a middle-aged man and his secretary in a hotel bedroom. The man is huddled under the bedclothes, wearing a troubled expression. His secretary, who is wearing rather less, is sitting up in bed beside him, taking shorthand dictation. Neither looks at the other. The caption reads: 'I'm sorry, Fiona, but it's the only way I can tell you how I feel . . .'

A final note. Although we have found several cartoons depicting female bosses, we have yet to find a single cartoon or joke about a male secretary. So much for sexual equality.

Secs scandals

At the very centre of one of the biggest political scandals in America this century – 'Irangate' – stood secretary Fawn Hall. It was she whom Lt Colonel Oliver North instructed to shred documents which might have provided vital evidence. As a result of the public investigation, Fawn Hall came out of her boss's shadow and became a public figure in her own right:

WHAM! IT'S LOVE AT FIRST SIGHT
NEW YORK: Pop star George Michael spotted America's most famous secretary across a crowded room – and fell in love.

The former singer with Wham! walked through a crowd of adoring women straight up to Irangate secretary Fawn Hall.

'She mesmerised me,' he said. 'She's not only beautiful, she's intelligent, witty, warm and fun.'

(*Sunday Express*, 19 February 1989)

Full marks to the *Sunday Express* for daring to present Fawn Hall as more than a stereotype. But straight to the bottom of the class goes *The People*, whose version of the same story ran like this:

GEORGE'S LOVE MOVE
Rock star George Michael has splashed out £2 million on a Hollywood mansion – so he can be near his new love, Irangate sexpot Fawn Hall.

All too often, the popular press present the secretary as part of the eternal power-sex-money triangle; and they see any story in which a rich and/or powerful man becomes involved with a secretary as a potential scandal. They like to depict the secretary as an office Mata Hari, out to manipulate the boss for her own gain; or else the fluffy blonde who would lie down and die for her boss – but more often than not it stops at the lying down . . . .

Nowhere is power a greater aphrodisiac than in politics, or so the press would have us believe. The liaisons between John Stonehouse and Sheila Buckley, Australian Premier John Gorton and Ainslie Gotto, Cecil Parkinson and Sara Keays all scandalized the public and caused political ruin or resignation.

The press and the committee investigating the Iran-Contra arms deals both tried very hard to prove an improper relationship between Oliver North and his secretary, Fawn Hall. North was alleged to have misappropriated White House funds to buy personal gifts for Miss Hall; and the press also made a great deal of capital out of the fact that she was an extremely attractive woman (whom men would presumably find hard to resist!). Throughout the investigations, Fawn Hall defended her boss to the hilt. In the end, no guilt attached to her and she emerged positively triumphant – in sharp contrast to her boss.

Why does it always appear to be the politicians who become involved with their secretaries, courting public disgrace? Is it anything to do with the type of women who are attracted to this allegedly glamorous type of secretarial work? Surely to suggest that all politicians' secretaries are potential mistresses is to cast an enormous slur upon the professionalism of the vast majority.

Probably just as many businessmen have affairs with their secretaries as do politicians. A close working relationship between the two sexes must by the law of averages result in some romantic attachments. The difference between business and politics is that business rarely captures the public imagination. It's exciting to read about politicians and their daring power-games, but much more exciting to read about politicians in disgrace.

Myth and reality

Fawn Hall, Miss Moneypenny, the wide-eyed damsels of romantic fiction and the dizzy blondes in cartoon strips – all are the stuff of public fantasy: but where does fantasy end and reality begin?

Take the following passage (from Radio 4's series, *King Street Junior*) as an example. Mrs Stone is portrayed as the organizational genius behind the day-to-day running of King Street Junior School; without her, the Headmaster (Mr Beeston) would quickly subside into helpless panic. Yet, in spite of this apparent power and influence, Mrs Stone is hardly a glamorous figure with an international jet-setting lifestyle:

> 'I've got the returns on the dinner figures. I've got the stock money to balance. I'm trying to type these letters to parents about the school trip. County Hall wants the insurance figures this afternoon.' Her voice was now rising as the catalogue of pressures on her built up. 'I've got teachers coming in here with all manner of things to be done: photocopies to be made, work sheets to be run off, letters to type. The phone keeps going. And with that drilling going on right outside my window . . . !'

Of course Mrs Stone is only a fictional character, though very well observed. But the Mrs Stones of the world outnumber the Fawn Halls several times over, despite the efforts of journalists and film producers to make us believe that the opposite is true.

No-one is saying that glamour cannot co-exist with secretarial work. Somebody has to be PA to Mrs Thatcher or Michael Jackson. But for most people, secretarial work is a profession with demanding standards and compensations which have nothing to do with hero-worship or sex. Today's career secretary has a host of myths to fight against in order to preserve his or her self-respect:

Myth	Reality
Secretaries are stupid.	Stupid secretaries are a contradiction in terms.
Secretaries are young and glamorous.	Many top-flight secretaries and PAs are in their forties and fifties. It's perfectly possible to be smart without looking like a Vogue model.
Secretaries are subservient.	Good secretaries are respected as professional members of the management team.
Secretaries and sex are synonymous.	Secretaries do not exist simply to tempt their bosses into office indiscretions. A professional will never allow personal considerations to affect his or her work.

These are just a few of the misconceptions which continue to thrive in spite of concerted attempts by professional associations to enhance the status and reputation of the private secretary. We are, frankly, appalled by the extent to which the secretary has apparently taken over from the nurse as the target for scandalmongering and sexist humour.

This chapter has been concerned with the myth of the secretary, and as such was designed to provoke, not to titillate. In our opinion secretaries remain remote and fascinating to most people because so little is known about what secretaries do. That's why the media get away with such outrageous stereotyping.

We hope that you, as a secretary, will agree that public awareness must be increased significantly if the record is ever to be put straight.

7

Training to be a Secretary

If you're already working as a secretary, you will know only too well that there's a lot more to the job than buying a blouse with a floppy white bow on the front.

And yet the title 'secretary' is as easily borrowed as a pair of sensible court shoes. How many times have you been infuriated to hear office juniors and page 3 models passing themselves off as 'secretaries' and devaluing the professionalism of the job? As one PA to a company Chairman told us: 'After I left college it was a good two or three years before I felt I could really call myself a secretary. It really annoys me to hear sixteen year-olds who think that just because they've done a course they're automatically secretaries.'

Unfortunately, the current status of secretaries is so poorly defined that they have no defence against the unqualified and inexperienced. Whereas it may be an offence to defraud the public by pretending to be a doctor or a policeman, no-one (to the best of our knowledge) has ever been prosecuted for impersonating a secretary!

Defining the status and role of a secretary has always posed problems, because of the absence of any national grading system or single series of examinations by which new entrants to the profession could be judged. Professional organizations like EAPS, IQPS and AMSPAR have all made valuable contributions by promoting secretarial work as a career and validating the professional qualifications of their own members. Yet the issue remains clouded, since so many junior office workers are graded as 'secretaries' simply to boost the image of the junior managers for whom they work.

Clerical assistants may feel flattered by the title of 'secretary', but unfortunately the lower the title sinks in the hierarchical structure, the less status and respect it attracts. Changes in office technology have also meant changes in the ways in which office staff work, their responsibilities and workload.

As working roles and relationships alter, so too must job titles and gradings. 1992 approaches fast and the Government –

recognizing the need for a national system of vocational training which will be accepted throughout Europe – has established the National Council for Vocational Qualifications. One by-product of the Council's overhaul of vocational qualifications may well be the necessity for a definitive statement about what really constitutes a secretary.

The status quo in basic training

If we had to pick a single word which best sums up the state of basic secretarial training today, it would have to be 'chaos'. The picture is of a system in flux, caught between old and new values, traditional examinations and the modern trend towards practical on-the-job assessments. Today's would-be secretary is faced with a bewildering array of training options: YTS, TVEI (Technical and Vocational Education Initiative), intensive 'skills' courses, formidable degree courses, day release courses . . . . All too often there's no-one impartial around to answer those all-important questions:

'Which is the best course for me?'
'Can I do better by going outside the area – and will I get a grant?'
'Will I be the only man on the course?'
'Will people laugh at me because I'm over forty?'
'What's the difference between RSA, LCCI and Pitman?'
'Do I really need shorthand? And which system should I learn?'

There's still so much ignorance about secretarial work that many sixteen-year-olds continue to believe that they can leave school with RSA I Typing and walk straight into a 'secretarial' job. They may be able to get a job as a junior typist, but the secretary's craft has to be learned – and that takes time and experience.

Not all trainee secretaries are sixteen-year-old girls, of course. Falling school rolls have provided employers with ample warning of an imminent sharp decline in the numbers of annual school leavers. Fierce competition has broken out amongst employers and training providers in an attempt to attract young people to one job or college rather than another. But this won't be enough. In order to keep their heads above water, employers need to supplement their pool of labour by casting their net more widely; women returners, the recently retired and men all need to be drawn into secretarial training if the present acute shortage of secretarial staff is not to worsen considerably.

One way of doing this is to enhance the image of secretarial work, to try to present it as a career which is just as worthwhile as teaching or engineering. In theory, increasing the academic content of some courses (e.g. upgrading to HND and BA level) helps to attract the attention of the more able students – people who would not even consider the job if course entrance requirements were, say, two GCSEs. Sustained demand for competent secretaries will also mean that salaries continue to improve all over the country. This could be instrumental in drawing in men and single parents who depend upon a good, steady wage to support their families.

NCVQ and the training revolution

In 1985 the Government decided to act upon the disturbing finding that only 40% of employees were properly qualified to do their jobs. The result was the establishment of the National Council for Vocational Qualifications. Comprising members of all the many interest groups (including Trade Unions), the Council was given the task of streamlining national vocational training provision to improve British qualifications and make them acceptable to employers throughout the European Community. Most important of all, qualifications accredited by NCVQ would indicate practical competence at doing a particular job, not just the ability to recall facts in an examination situation.

Oscar DeVille, present Chairman of NCVQ, was quoted in a *Times* article (10 March 1989) as saying this:

> We want more training, and flexibility. We do not want to stifle initiative. We do not want to undermine things that are good (. . .). It means that people will be able to see their prospects more clearly (so will parents). People in education will be clearer about ladders of progression, and employers in particular should find out that qualifications that bear our stamp mean that people are competent to be employed.

In practical terms, all vocational qualifications will be standardized nationally into graded levels of attainment. Each level will consist of a number of units, which may be taken all at once or separately, perhaps with months or even years between them, under different validating bodies and in different parts of the country. When trainees have accumulated the full complement of units for a given level, they send off their certificates to one validating body (say RSA or LCCI) which will exchange them for a full NVQ [National Vocational Qualification] certificate for that level. Margaret Evans is Senior Examinations Officer (Secretarial Studies) at the London Chamber of Commerce and Industry. She feels that the new developments are long overdue and welcomes both the modular structure of NVQs and their emphasis on practical competence:

> It's wonderful that you are not penalized if you move. This way, you can be very flexible: you can choose to do the units that you identify as giving you the best chance of employment in a given area (. . .). As a former professional secretary myself, I am also pleased that for the first few years after school or college, people will still be studying for their units: so they won't actually be secretaries until they have learned the job.

It's anticipated that NVQs will be fully implemented up to level 3 (first-line management) by 1992. Secretarial training will be included within the 'Business Administration' classification; but it's felt that no-one possessing a qualification below level 3 will have sufficient knowledge, skills or experience to merit the title of 'secretary'. This is why the word 'secretarial' will not appear in documentation for Business Administration level 1 or 2.

As an approximate guide, it's likely that NVQ level 3 will be of a similar standard to the present LCCI Private Secretary's Certificate; but there will be no real equivalents since formal examinations will no longer exist and practical experience will carry considerable weight in obtaining qualifications. Specialist secretarial training (e.g. medical) is also likely to start at level 3, and in the future secretarial qualifications may extend upwards to level 6 (which would be above the level of a first degree).

So in theory at least no-one with less than NVQ level 3 ought to be graded as a secretary. This could cause quite a stir in organizations which currently employ large numbers of 'secretaries' who are really no more than receptionists, typists or word processor operators. As Margaret Evans points out: 'NVQs will identify the qualification-holder rather than the post.' This means that for the very first time secretaries have a chance of obtaining a proper graded career structure based on their own qualifications and experience rather than on the seniority and promotion prospects of their managers. A situation could even arise in which a secretary with grade 4 qualifications worked for, say, an accountant or engineer whose NVQ level was only 3 – and the secretary would have every justification for demanding a higher salary than the manager!

Miss Evans feels that limiting true secretarial qualifications to NVQ level 3 and above will persuade employers to take a closer look at their present staff gradings, and may induce them to downgrade those posts which aren't really secretarial at all. A level 3 secretary will demand a level 3 salary, so it's not in employers' interests to allow the designation to drift too far downwards through the office hierarchy, if only to limit wage demands! On the plus side, limiting the use of the title 'secretary' may – in the long run – enhance its prestige and so attract more trainees.

Much of NVQ training will link theory to practical skills and problem situations. Indeed, it looks as if many employers and private employment agencies will take up the challenge to become trainers and assessors in their own right, in direct competition with the struggling LEA colleges. It makes good sense for employers to arrange for their secretarial employees to be assessed on the job, as real problem situations arise, rather than for the secretaries to be sent to colleges which then have to simulate complex situations for assessment purposes.

Some people – particularly within the Trade Union movement – are worried that employers will wield too much power over their employees as on-the-job training grows in importance. As Margaret Evans explains:

> The higher up you get, you really have got to have (I would say) a supportive employer: or the college that you go to to get the training has got to have a very good relationship with the local employer in order to allow a complete stranger to come in and do high-level work. In order to satisfy some of the requirements of level 4, someone is going to have to give you access to a Board meeting, and they simply aren't going to do it. So that is why I say that employers are going to have quite a lot of control.

Some Trade Unionists feel that, if employers control training, they will ensure that their employees only train in those areas which are specifically useful to the organization at that time. It might also be in a firm's interests to block an employee's attempts to obtain all the units for the next NVQ level – as this would probably mean having to pay that employee a higher salary on qualification.

On the positive side, really gifted secretaries whose worth is appreciated by their bosses may be able to use training as a bargaining point: 'I'll work for you, but only if you sponsor me for level 4', and so on. If employers are unsympathetic, then some of the larger employment agencies such as Alfred Marks may step into the breach and provide training on weekday evenings. Many of them already have their own custom-built training centres and are only waiting for the right moment to grab a bigger share of the secretarial training market.

The students have their say

Books about secretaries tend either to talk in abstract terms or are designed as textbooks for the (apparently) devoted student of secretarial work. Nobody ever seems to ask students what they think, do and would like to happen; and we felt it was time to put the record straight.

We decided to carry out an informal survey of students currently attending a variety of different colleges in England, both private and maintained. A total of 232 completed questionnaires were returned, from the following colleges:

Private sector

Pitman College: six-month and one-year intensive secretarial courses

St Godric's College: one-year executive secretarial course

Lucie Clayton College: six-month and one-year secretarial courses

Public sector

Newcastle Polytechnic: BA Secretarial Studies

Humberside Business School (Hull): BA Office Systems Management and HND Business Studies (secretarial option)

Merton College (London SW20): one-year intensive secretarial course

Scarborough Technical College: one-year LCCI Secretarial
Studies Certificate Course;
Year One and Year Two of two-year LCCI Private
Secretary's Certificate Course;
One-year Advanced Secretarial Course (leading to LCCI
Private Secretary's Certificate).

All 232 students who completed our questionnaire were female,
which we found rather disappointing. The national press is full of
stories of high-flying male secretaries and PAs, so we can only
conclude either that they all train somewhere else or that they don't
like filling in questionnaires! (Most of the top male PAs we have
encountered have in fact not been secretarial-trained at all, but are
young business school graduates seconded to the Chairman's office
as the first step in a brilliant management career.)

The age range of the students was sixteen to forty-three, with
89% aged twenty-one or under. Several of the older students were
from overseas, and had been seconded for in-service training. The
college with the broadest age range was Scarborough (16–43),
whilst at Merton all students were aged between sixteen and
nineteen.

Entrance qualifications ranged from hardly any qualifications at
all (a couple of CSEs and RSA I typing) to four 'A' levels, a degree
and a teacher's certificate. Most of the students had gained relevant
work experience, either prior to the course or on work placements
during their studies. Understandably, the short courses devoted
little time to work experience.

The fairly narrow age range of most students and the lack of male
respondents prompts us to ask whether colleges are trying hard
enough to attract mature and male secretarial students to their
courses in a period when sixteen-to twenty-one-year-old trainees
are at a premium.

Choosing a college

We asked students to give their main reasons for choosing their
particular college. The responses were as follows:

location	29%
reputation	26%

appeared to offer a good course	23%
only option/last resort	6%

A large number of students appeared to have selected their college simply because it was the nearest one to home. Surprisingly this included some of those on the BA course at Newcastle Polytechnic. 46% cited location as a major factor (either proximity to home or facilities offered in the city), as against 62% who selected the course as the main reason. Since the course at Newcastle is the only one of its kind in the country, it's not surprising that this scored highly in the questionnaire. On the other hand, 78% of those who gave 'last resort' or 'only option' as a reason were at Newcastle! This might suggest that some students selected the BA Secretarial Studies course as a second-choice business studies degree, rather than out of a positive desire to become secretaries.

Although all the students who participated in our survey could be said to be following secretarial courses (with the possible exception of the Office Systems Management students at Hull), their syllabuses and daily routines differed widely from college to college. We asked students to prepare 'diaries' of their typical college day and quote examples (one from a maintained college, one from a private college) at the end of this chapter. We think they illustrate the differences of emphasis and environment very well, and would like to thank the authors for the time and trouble they spent in committing their thoughts to paper.

Choosing a course

We then asked the students, 'Why did you choose this course?' The responses were as follows:

because it was vocational/provided useful skills for employment	35%
because it looked interesting	24%
because Business Studies were included	6%
because I wanted to be a secretary	6%
to get a good/better job	5%

It is interesting to note that whilst students were evidently highly motivated by the prospect of obtaining employment only 6% specified that they took the course because they wanted to be secretaries.

Course content

There were huge variations in course content, although all students took some shorthand and keyboarding skills and most also had some instruction in word processing.

Lucie Clayton College, Newcastle Polytechnic and (not surprisingly) Pitman College favoured Pitman 2000 New Era shorthand, with Scarborough, Merton, St Godric's and Humberside all opting for Teeline. We were quite surprised that Newcastle taught Pitman shorthand, since the demands of the degree course leave only a few hours per week for shorthand tuition and Pitman is a notoriously slow system to master. Time spent on 'skills' subjects varied immensely, depending on the length of the course. For example, whereas students at Newcastle spent perhaps three hours per week on shorthand, students on the six-month intensive course at Pitman College spent anything between eight and seventeen hours per week learning the same system.

Most colleges made some attempt to include business-related subjects in their timetable. Most heavily business-oriented were Newcastle, Hull, Scarborough and St Godric's, with Lucie Clayton and Merton College lagging rather a long way behind with perhaps only forty-five minutes per week.

Other subjects included computer literacy (spreadsheets and databases), accounts, law, medical reception duties, communications, secretarial duties, audio-typing, current affairs, journalism, advertising and management. Perhaps least conventional was the Lucie Clayton emphasis on self-presentation (grooming, deportment) and 'fringe' subjects such as flower-arranging and art appreciation.

We asked the students which subjects they found most useful, which were least useful and which they would like to see added to their courses. The results were as follows:

Most useful subjects

keyboarding/typing	24%
shorthand	19%
word processing	12%
Information Technology/computing skills	6%
foreign languages for business	6%
communications	5%

Even among the degree-course students, the basic 'skills' were felt to be the most useful element of the course.

Least useful subjects

all subjects are useful	25%
business studies	10%
international business	6%
management	5%
secretarial duties/office practice	5%
shorthand	4%

Many students expressed a desire to go into management or to run their own businesses, and fifteen out of thirty-one students at St Godric's claimed to have chosen the course because it contained business studies – yet the three most unpopular subjects turned out to be business studies, international business and management! We suspect that this has something to do with the quality of teaching or the scarcity of suitable *secretarial* learning materials which can help illustrate the relevance of these subjects to secretarial work.

Preferred additions to syllabus

no additions needed	46%
(more) accounts/book-keeping	8%
(more) practical office procedures	5%
(more) audio-typing	4%
telephone/reception skills	4%
grooming/deportment	4%

Getting a job

Since students were evidently motivated by the prospect of gaining useful skills for employment, we were interested in finding out how they proposed to find a suitable job at the end of their course. Their responses were distributed as follows:

newspaper advertisements	29%
employment agencies (permanent work)	20%
personal contacts	18%
college careers service	17%
employment agencies (temporary work)	14%
other (e.g. Job Centre, speculative letters)	1%
don't know	1%

We were interested to note the relative importance of personal contacts across the board. This factor was certainly not confined to the private sector, where students might be expected to have access to 'privileged' contacts. Only two students out of 232 were considering sending out speculative letters to potential employers.

The most popular areas of employment were the so-called 'glamour' areas such as PR, advertising and publishing. Medical and financial work lagged well behind general secretarial and PA posts, although legal secretarial work was rated quite highly in career terms. Agricultural secretarial work did not feature at all.

Another interesting point to note is the relative unpopularity of temping. Only 13% said that they would consider temping as a career. 15% stated that they might temp in order to try out different types of work before settling down to a permanent post. But a massive 63% had no intention of looking for anything other than full-time, permanent work from the outset.

When asked how long they expected to spend in their first job, the largest group of responses lay in the area of one to two years (36%), though responses did vary between 'a couple of months' and 'more than five years' or 'as long as possible'. There appeared to be no significant regional variations, despite the greater opportunities for job mobility and salary increases in the South East.

Students' salary expectations in their first jobs did, however, display considerable variations both according to levels of attainment and geographical area. The most frequently quoted salary band was £8,500–£10,500, which accounted for 41%. However, 15% of students expected to earn £12,000 or more per annum – the majority of them students on the BA course at Newcastle. This is perhaps not surprising, since these students will be exceptionally well qualified and will presumably be seeking employment all over the UK. At the other end of the scale, 59% of the Scarborough students expected to earn £6,000 or less per year – 26% of them expected to earn £5,000 or less. Scarborough is situated in a rural area with limited (and often seasonal) employment opportunities, and wages for secretaries are notoriously low – quite a contrast to the glamorous image portrayed by secretarial employment agencies in London.

65% of students said that they would prefer to work for one boss rather than several. Many felt that this would allow a better working atmosphere to develop, and that receiving instructions from only one person would help eliminate conflicts of interest and confusion. To quote one respondent: 'Having one person telling me what to do is bad enough!' It was also believed by some that promotion prospects would be better, since one-to-one experience would be a good grounding for PA and management assistant posts. Only 13% would prefer to work for more than one boss (citing variety as the reason for their choice).

75% of students claimed that the age and sex of their boss did not matter to them. However, 13% said that they would prefer to work for a man, whereas only 2% would prefer a female manager.

Pros and cons

We asked our respondents to list what they felt to be the main advantages and disadvantages of being a secretary. The results were as follows:

Advantages

plenty of jobs/mobility	17%
money	13%
variety of work	9%
stepping stone to other jobs	9%
job satisfaction	4%
travel	4%
opportunity to use skills	4%

It is interesting that three of the top four advantages are expressed in somewhat negative terms: having plenty of work and earning money whilst waiting for 'something better' to turn up. Relatively few students felt inspired by the actual content of the job itself.

Disadvantages

poor public image/stereotyping	19%
boredom, monotonous work	18%
feeling of inferiority, low status	11%
being taken for granted	8%
limited salary	7%
being told what to do all the time	5%
the boss gets all the credit	5%

The main threads here seemed to be sensitivity to the public perception of secretaries as brainless blondes and a feeling on the part of students that the secretary was at best a subordinate figure, not a member of the management team. The words 'bimbo' and 'sex object' were wielded with much righteous indignation in many questionnaires.

The perfect secretary

Students were asked to list the qualities which they considered most important in a good secretary. The most frequently occurring qualities are listed below:

efficiency: (67 responses)	11%
organizational skills (58)	10%
pleasant personality, friendliness (36)	6%
good 'skills' (shorthand, typing, WP) (34)	6%
smart appearance, good grooming (28)	5%
patience (27)	5%
good manners, politeness (23)	4%
reliability (22)	4%
common sense (17)	3%
initiative, self-motivation (16)	3%
maturity, responsible attitude (16)	3%

Secretaries and careers

We then asked students if they would be seeking secretarial employment at the end of their course. Despite their doubts about the image and prospects of the job the majority (57%) said 'Yes'. 26% said they wouldn't be looking for a secretarial job, with the remainder either undecided or planning to move on after a year or two.

The responses to the question: 'Do you intend to stay in secretarial work or move on to something else?' were as follows:

move on	60%
not going into secretarial work at all	8%
undecided	16%
stay in secretarial work	15%

From these results it was clear that 68% had no intention of making a long-term career in secretarial work – rather high wastage for students who were supposedly training to become secretaries. Students with lower entrance qualifications seemed to have a more long-term view of secretarial work than those on high-level courses. For example, only 10% of Merton College's students (who were of post-GCSE standard) definitely planned to move on, with the figure rising to 31% at Scarborough. At the other end of the scale, 82% of Newcastle's undergraduate students had no intention of remaining in secretarial work. Hull's BA students clearly felt that their Office Systems Management course (despite its secretarial skills content) fitted them for 'higher things'; 89% of them wanted to get out of secretarial work even before they had begun. To quote one Hull student: 'I would not wish to undervalue myself.'

It was with some trepidation, therefore, that we asked the question: 'Is secretarial work a career?' To our surprise the answer was an overwhelming 'Yes' from 70% as opposed to 19% who thought it was not. However it was a qualified 'Yes' in many cases and we also felt that there was some confusion about what a career really was. In some cases respondents assumed that any reasonably secure job with a regular salary was a career, irrespective of whether or not it possessed any formal career structure. This resulted in many people saying that secretarial work was a career and on the next page complaining because it hadn't got a career structure! Bearing in mind the high proportion of respondents who intended to move out of secretarial work, the results can be summed up in the words of one respondent: 'Yes, it's a career – but not for me.'

Ideals and ambitions

Finally, we asked students to tell us about their hopes for the future – their career ambitions and (just for fun) the people they would really like to work for.

Career ambitions ranged from the near-impossible ('to be Secretary General of the United Nations') to the homely ('to be extremely boring and marry the man I love and raise a family – which I consider to be a very good career!'). Most were challenging and centred on hopes of power, wealth, status and success. Only eleven students specifically wanted to be secretaries, whilst twenty thought they might like to be PAs – mostly to famous people or captains of industry. Fifty-four students wanted to go into management, whilst thirty-five wanted to be 'rich and successful' and twenty-one were determined to run their own businesses. The remainder selected a variety of non-secretarial careers of professional standing, for example engineering, teaching, journalism, copywriting, systems analysis.

When asked to name their 'ideal boss' our respondents leaned heavily towards well-known media figures. No fewer than twenty different people from pop music, TV and films were listed, including Tom Cruise (3), Richard Gere, Steven Spielberg and Mel Gibson. Five students opted for members of the Royal Family, and politicians also featured (John Smith, Neil Kinnock, Michael Heseltine . . . and of course, Margaret Thatcher, who attracted three votes). Entrepreneurs chosen included Sir Terence Conran, Anita Roddick, Ralph Halpern and Alan Sugar. Other choices included: the Saatchi brothers, the Pope, the head of the UK Porsche empire, the Editor of *Kerrang!*, Imelda Marcos, the head of the Metropolitan Police, and the cast of *Neighbours*. Streets ahead of his rivals, with no fewer than twelve votes, was Richard Branson, head of the Virgin empire. His combination of youthful approach, glamorous lifestyle, wealth, rock music, leisure and power proved irresistible to students in all the colleges participating in our survey.

Strangely enough, very few of the 'ideal' bosses were female; it seems that female secretaries really are reluctant to work for other women, at least initially. A few students did, however, select female bosses, including one student from Merton College who announced that her ideal boss was: 'My mother. She wouldn't take advantage of me or shout if I am late and she would want to pay me heaps.'

Our conclusions

First of all we should perhaps emphasize that we don't claim to be statisticians; ours was an entirely informal survey, dependent upon the cooperation of a relatively small number of students and their tutors. However, we do feel that within their obvious limitations the survey results are valid.

Within the limited time available to us, we made every effort to ensure that our sample included students attending both private and maintained colleges in London and the North, and studying for qualifications ranging from a handful of RSA skills certificates to a full BA degree in Secretarial Studies. Whilst we would not attempt to draw national generalizations from the results of our survey, we believe that they do serve to illustrate a number of important themes and trends:

1 There were no men and few mature students in our sample. This could have something to do with the poor public image of secretarial work, which was mentioned by many respondents. Colleges and professional bodies will have to try harder if they are going to attract more people to an area of work which is already suffering from serious staff shortages;

2 Many of our respondents appeared to be taking a secretarial course as a means of doing something else (the 'back door' to another career), or as a last resort following poor examination results. This trend is rather alarming, since such a high level of wastage offers little prospect of alleviating secretarial staff shortages;

3 Those students following degree courses were very keen *not* to become secretaries, even though Newcastle students were supposedly being trained in 'secretarial studies'. Since many managers remain unwilling to employ graduates as secretaries, we found ourselves wondering whether degree-level studies are really a fitting foundation for a career in secretarial work;

4 There was widespread discontent about the lack of a formal career structure for secretaries. Hopefully, the reform of vocational training instigated by NCVQ will go some way towards providing at least a proper grading system for secretaries, leading to improvements in status;

5 A word about presentation. Around 44% of all completed questionnaires contained errors of grammar and/or spelling. Even allowing for errors resulting from haste this is worrying. After all, these are tomorrow's professional administrators and communicators – and tomorrow's managers too, if their ambitions are realistic! They need to have an excellent command of English to do their jobs properly, but in many of them this proved to be sadly lacking, as this selection of 'howlers' illustrates:

– 'one has to have a good knowledge of *english* and *grammer*'
– 'then we have *excersizes*'
– '*Pittman* New Era shorthand'
– '*Brittish*'
– 'secretarial work is a *confident* and *prospectous* career'
– 'other *secretary's* you work with'
– 'a more *diversed* range'

- '*indispendable*'
- 'a woman can do a job as *good* as a man'
- 'you need *patients*, so I'd be no good'
- 'at the end of the course I will be well *quailified*'
- 'someone who knows what *your* thinking'
- 'secretarial work gives a general *incite* into the running of businesses'
- 'a secretary must be someone who is *punctuate*'
- 'my ambition is to learn as *much* different languages as possible and to work as a secretary with foreign *correspondences* in the firm'
- '*efficiantcy*'
- '*entrepenure*'
- 'I'd stay there till I got *use* to the place.'

Student diaries

Scarborough Technical College

Vanessa Snowden (Secretarial Studies Certificate Course): I can definitely say that I have changed since I started this course. When I was at school I didn't seem to realize how it was going to affect my future. Then I decided upon the course I am undertaking at the moment and everything is so different, for I am being taught and treated like an adult. It is such a large step from school but I am glad I have taken it. I actually feel that if I contribute something to the group, no matter how small, it is noticed by everybody.

Scarborough Technical College has made a vast change in my life. It has given me the chance to mix with different age groups and feel relaxed among strangers. It has also given me confidence within myself.

Simone Rackley (Private Secretary's Certificate Course, Year Two):
A typical day in the Business Studies Department:
At around 8.55 am members of the PSC group arrive one by one after fighting over spaces in the student car park. It's a Monday morning and at 9.00 am the first lesson is Structure of Business, so we all have to try and find our teacher in one of the mobile classrooms. We usually assemble somewhere outside in view of all three and freeze until the teacher arrives to let us in.

As soon as we have set foot inside the classroom it is straight down to the Balance of Payments and International Trade. While the teacher tries to put everything in the most logical way possible, we all try to look as if we fully understand what he is talking about.

Eventually, 10.00 am creeps round and we all troop up to the fourth floor, where the majority of our lessons are held. Room 49 – Communications. After standing in the corridor for a few minutes our teacher arrives, muttering something about having to make a telephone call and looking slightly harassed. A quick moan when he announces we've yet another summary to do, as we 'still haven't really got the hang of them', and we settle down to work.

10.45 am: Break time! About fifteen of us try and cram into one lift – although the maximum load is ten – and we all go along to the Refectory and see how many cartons of milk and packets of crisps we can consume in fifteen minutes.

11.00 am: Back up to the 4th floor for Secretarial Procedures. The teacher is never late. She is usually already there, standing with her overhead projector and a load of notes about banking facilities or arranging conferences for us to read, copy down and inwardly digest.

Lunch time at last! A lot of our group have cars, so most of them go into town or home. 12.00–1.00 pm is the only hour of the day that seems to go quickly.

On a Monday afternoon, half of the group work in the TVEI office, which usually means working on Apple Mac computers. There is usually a debate each week about which half of the group's turn it is to go into the office.

In the office we get the opportunity to use a laser printer, which – in comparison with ordinary daisy wheel and dot matrix printers – produces really good quality print.

Monday afternoon seems to last for hours! But eventually 4.00 pm comes round. Tomorrow we've got shorthand, information processing and an option of either French, legal secretarial or medical reception to look forward to – which takes us right up to 7.30 pm. So Monday doesn't seem so bad after all!

Lucie Clayton Secretarial College

A day in the life of Heather Addison: It is a great relief when I am actually inside the College; I have spent an hour travelling, and when the weather is cold the walk up from Gloucester Road Tube

Station is a miserable one. I leave home at 8.40 am and arrive in Kensington approximately an hour later.

The College is situated in a very elegant terrace and is very glamorous inside: red carpets, attractive wallpaper and chandeliers. Down a flight of stairs to the cloakroom, leave my coat on a hanger, then begin my climb up five flights of stairs to my form room. Classes are in pairs because there is a typing room and a shorthand room: you alternate rooms with your parallel class. On our floor are the make-up room and two bathrooms. Upstairs are the word processing room and another typing and shorthand room. On a Wednesday Mrs Broke-Smith weighs the girls who participate in the diet club. I go up to find this week I have not lost any weight: I am annoyed! The boarder girls have their bedrooms on the two top floors.

My first lesson is shorthand. Our floor is on early break this week, so our first lesson lasts one hour ten minutes. Over the next two weeks we are studying 700 common words (which make up 70% of the average dictation passage). Today is our third section of fifty words. We study and take note of them, then for homework we will drill and learn them. We completed all the Pitman New Era theory last term. These next two terms we concentrate on speed.

We are dismissed and all go down to the Buttery with the other class on our floor. The Buttery is where we are allowed to eat and drink. It is like a common room, with a television for the boarder girls. I get a coffee (no sugar) from the machine (from which you can have practically any drink of your choice).

At approximately 11.20 am we start to make our way upstairs (the Buttery is in the basement and at Christmas, on the last day of term, we had mince pies and a glass of wine down there). The next lesson is typing. Our timetable mostly alternates between typing and shorthand and every week we have a different set of lectures, not in any regular weekly format. We all go to our usual seats and get to work. There are fourteen in my class. We all proceed individually through set work. Marks are always taken and put towards our weekly report. Today there is no time left for a speed test. We had an afternoon of speed tests recently and I managed 69 words a minute, which I was pleased with as I still have a term and three quarters to go.

1 pm: time for lunch. Around the college there are numerous wine bars, pizzerias and bistros – we vary where we go. Today, for a

change, four of us go to Pizzaland at Earls Court. One stop on the tube and we are able to get there, eat and get back just within the hour.

Straight down to the changing room. We all get kitted up: leotards, ankle warmers and jazz shoes! Up three flights of stairs past the mirrored wall to the 'Green Room', the main room where the catwalk lives, surrounded by impeccable décor! Forty-five minutes of extremely vigorous exercise to loud music. We know it is good for us but it is still painful. Cool down, whizz downstairs and we change back to our normal garments.

Our class is divided into two groups. Half go to a deportment lesson. I am in the half that begins with make-up (after twenty minutes we change over). In make-up today we are taught how to do a quick quarter-of-an-hour routine for the morning: a light foundation, powder, eyes, blusher and lips. Other lessons have concentrated on one style or area of the face. Anne-Marie (who is our make-up teacher and also a dermatologist) said I could go to her at break tomorrow to have my eyebrows plucked again. I note this down in my Fax.

We leave the make-up room, which resembles a theatrical dressing-room designed for ten people. Changeover time, and for the next twenty minutes or so, up to 4.30 pm, I have deportment with Mrs Broke-Smith, an ex-model. A hasty trip down a flight of stairs and one flight of the back spiral staircase to go to the Drawing Room. First, we all individually recap the previous lessons: walking, the Paris turn, entering and exiting a room without turning your back on everybody, and how to sit down. Today we learn the full catwalk turn, the normal turn (180°) and how to take a coat off and put it on without hitting everyone around you, losing a sleeve or dropping it. The Drawing Room is a relaxing, mirrored room with an elegant fireplace and large windows overlooking the gardens. Mrs Broke-Smith says that next lesson we will be put on video so we can watch ourselves walk and hopefully learn from seeing our mistakes on the catwalk.

4.30 pm: hometime. We go down to retrieve our coats then brave the cold to return home – where we can then recharge our batteries, study our shorthand and get prepared for the next Lucie Clayton day.

8

A Successful Secretary for Today and Tomorrow

Yesterday's secretary looks back: Memoirs of a Wrinkly Sec by 'Marjorie'

Many years before the invention of Tipp-Ex or electric typewriters I started my secretarial career after four years' training at a Central School, emerging at the age of sixteen with certificates in shorthand (100 wpm) and typewriting (30 wpm).

Jobs were scarce, but I secured one at the usual rate of twenty-five shillings per week and travelled up to the City each day, neatly dressed complete with gloves and hat. Office hours were nine till six, with a half day on Saturday: but if the boss asked you to do overtime this was unpaid, and people were frightened to refuse for fear of losing their jobs.

My best friend worked for an old firm in Newgate Street, where make-up was taboo and dresses had to have high necks and long sleeves! Nonetheless, the older men in the office had all married their typists and of course, marriage meant instant dismissal. If a girl was married it was a closely guarded secret and she kept her maiden name.

In my first secretarial position I was told to sweep the office floor in the morning. At lunchtime I had to carry three-course meals for my employer and his lady friend up four flights of stairs from a ground-floor restaurant – and then go down for coffee. This state of affairs did not last long as Scotland Yard had their eye on my boss and his associates, and they all finished up in prison for fraud. I had to give evidence at the Old Bailey.

In my second job at an engineering firm my friend and I worked very hard indeed and were in terror of the boss, who thundered out instructions through a Dictaphone on our desks. This did our nerves no good at all, and we made many erasures and often stuck small patches on the letters to cover the holes – all to no avail: they had to be typed and retyped many times.

There was no chance of an increase in pay, so I left to work for an Air Ministry outstation which was taking on extra staff owing to the threat of war. At first I worked for a Flight Lieutenant who insisted I bring him a glass of hot milk every hour as he had a stomach ulcer – but otherwise all my bosses were pleasant enough, although we all lived in fear of the charlady whose wrath knew no bounds when she discovered my bicycle tyre marks on *her* highly-polished floor.

When war broke out I volunteered to transfer to the Air Ministry at Whitehall. Labour was scarce because of the call-up and it was quite in order for married women to work. I found myself working for high-ranking officers who needed to dictate almost round the clock; so we shorthand-typists started at 3 pm and worked until 3 pm the next day, when we went home. Of course, we were allowed to sleep far below ground, but had to remain on call in case urgent work materialized. Sometimes we had to bash out twenty copies of our work for the Chiefs of Staff on incredibly thin paper. At other times, we typed out huge schedules to do with the proposed invasion of Europe, which required us to glue together four sheets of the largest-sized paper. Quite often our bosses were standing at our elbow, impatiently ripping out the sheets from our machines to rush off to an even higher-ranking officer who, they said, was 'screaming for it'!

Many years later, after marrying and bringing up a family, I returned to work as a City temp. I found most of my bosses kind and considerate with a few exceptions, like the man at the Royal Mint who dictated with his head stuck out of the window; or the engineering boss who invariably left work to the very last minute so that I had to type with motorbike and despatch rider at my side, ready to rush off to the other end of the country!

I could write much more about the interesting and sometimes charming people I have worked for, and I really miss the whole scene now that I am at home all the time. One thing is certain: a difficult boss needs to be handled tactfully and with infinite patience. He is most likely suffering from stress and will soon realize how indispensable you are. As everything in offices speeds up, it seems to me that more is expected from us all – but we must do our best to remain calm and serene.

Today's top secretaries

The following is an extract from a press release issued by Reed Employment in April 1988:

BOSSES – MANAGEMENT TAKEOVER BID BY BRITISH SECRETARIES!

According to a new survey by leading recruitment agency Reed Employment, today's secretaries are better trained and more ambitious than ever before. They have got plenty of ideas on how to improve office efficiency, and more than three quarters of those who took part in the survey have got their sights set on promotion.

The message seems to be that today's secretaries are aiming for the top; and as part of their master plan for promotion, they are taking on more of a managerial role. This means more responsibility, and greater control over the organization's resources: time, people, money and information.

Since secretarial salaries – at least in the South East – are high and rising, it might be thought that secretaries were motivated mainly by money. This assumption is strongly contested by the results of a survey carried out by the Industrial Society in 1987. *Secretaries: A wasted asset?* contains interesting information on what secretaries claim really motivates them. The results were as follows:

challenge and responsibility	45%
job involvement	43%
salary	12%

Salary comes a very poor third, and of those who claimed to be motivated by money 21% were involved in the banking and finance sectors (where salaries and benefits such as subsidized mortgages are particularly attractive).

Judging from these statistics, what the modern secretary is looking for is a job which offers a chance to prove what he or she can do, and which will involve the secretary in every aspect of the business. Modern secretaries actively seek out the burdens of knowledge and decision-making.

The perfect secretary?

What do bosses really want from a secretary? A business partner; a *confidante*; a status symbol?

Employment agencies know only to well that it's in their interests to find out the sort of secretary bosses want so that they can provide the right 'product'. Mackay Personnel have produced a booklet entitled *The Perfect Secretary*, in which they list 'Ten attributes that add up to the sort of secretary every business executive needs':

- skills
- intelligence
- efficiency
- acceptance of responsibility
- initiative
- loyalty
- dedication
- grooming
- tact
- charm

The list appears to be divided evenly between 'positive' or 'masculine' qualities such as initiative and acceptance of responsibility and 'negative' or 'feminine' qualities such as dedication and charm. The perfect secretary, according to Mackay Personnel, has to tread a rather narrow tightrope between tact and initiative, efficiency and charm.

In 1981 Alfred Marks published the results of an international survey into employers' requirements, *The Ideal Secretary*. At that time responses indicated that employers preferred their secretaries to be:

- young (25–30)
- female (53% of UK employers said they would not employ male secretaries)
- not too highly qualified (only 7% preferred graduate secretaries, and 93% said secretaries did not need any second language)

Other factors indicated were marital status, looks and personality. When asked to sum up the boss/secretary relationship, 58% described the secretary as a 'personal assistant', with 23% preferring 'all round helper'. Only 2% admitted to viewing their secretary as a '*confidante* and potential social companion'!

Today the indications are that bosses still prefer younger

secretaries. Such are the difficulties experienced by older women in obtaining secretarial employment that they have acquired their own acronym: TOAFFs ('Too old at forty-fives'). An article entitled 'Finished at 45' (*Weekend*, 3 December 1988) outlines the problem clearly. Michael Yorke, marketing director of Reed Employment, is quoted as saying: 'It's a question of attitude. Employers have an idealistic view of what they want. In the case of a secretary it's someone aged twenty to thirty and female.'

The respondents to the 1981 survey were not at all comfortable with the idea of male secretaries. To quote the survey, 'Amongst the reasons given were that they would miss "femininity" and that they would feel embarrassed at giving him dictation or sending him on errands. In . . . the UK and the USA, the external impression created by employing a male secretary was of major concern.'

The situation has changed quite considerably. Reeds now report that one in every twenty applicants for secretarial work is male, and we are told that a new breed of high-powered, computer-literate male 'sec-exec' is ready to turn the world of secretarial work upside-down. There is little evidence of quite such a revolution at the moment, but female secretaries had better not rest on their laurels if they want to remain dominant in the job market.

If we accept the list of qualities supplied by Mackay Personnel as the basic requirement for a 'perfect' secretary, is there anything we can add to it to bring it up to date? We would certainly suggest that any secretary aiming for the top today should be thinking in terms of computer training: not just word processing, but databases, spread-sheets and even desktop publishing. The secretary who is fully computer literate will always be in a position of power, since most bosses simply don't have the time to learn very much about new technology themselves.

June Tatum, President of the Executive Secretaries' Club, would also advise any secretary who wants to maximize his or her potential to take post-basic courses, perhaps in economics or management. This might well help if you want to get out of secretarial work, but it's as well to remember that bosses are still vaguely uneasy about highly-qualified secretaries. If you want to develop your career within secretarial work, it might be wise to concentrate on gaining experience rather than too many certificates, to avoid pricing yourself out of the market.

A changing profession

Secretarial work is a career in flux. Secretaries stand on the brink of management, carrying out many managerial tasks and working alongside senior managers every day – yet they're still not widely accepted as managers in their own right.

Technology is also turning the job inside out. It's no longer possible to leave work, bring up a family and return to work ten years later with no more than a quick shorthand refresher course. Offices today are unrecognizable in terms of offices a decade ago; and the pace of change looks like accelerating rather than slowing down. The secretary, like the nurse, has been forced to become a skilled technician simply in order to keep on top of the job, and regular retraining is becoming an integral part of almost everyone's working life.

Yet whilst salaries boom and electronic offices take over the South of England, there are still areas of the country in which salaries are low, prospects non-existent and working conditions primitive: the manual typewriter refuses to die without a fight! And it's worth remembering that there will always be secretaries in small businesses whose jobs do not conform to national high-tech stereotypes.

As far as stereotypes go, our survey of the media has suggested that whilst newspapers are happy to fascinate us with tales of high life and champagne for £30,000-a-year PAs, the popular image of the secretary is still that of the brainless blonde. It doesn't yet appear to have come to terms with the male secretary at all!

Secretaries for tomorrow

Our research has highlighted the following trends:

- **Training**: the full implementation of National Vocational Qualifications by the mid-1990s will turn present training provision on its head. Colleges will have to compete with employers for trainees as secretarial training becomes far more work-based. The modular nature of NVQs should encourage trainees to study over longer periods and so gain both qualifications and experience simultaneously.
- **Status and grading**: since only those with NVQ level 3 or above

will really have secretarial qualifications at all, it's possible that the title 'secretary' will return to favour. If jobs are graded strictly according to the qualification holder, there will inevitably be regrading of all office jobs on a massive scale. Gone will be the days of the typist who was called a secretary because it made her boss feel important.

- **Skills**: the skills which tomorrow's successful secretary will need are WP, IP, administrative skills, business knowledge, and management skills – but shorthand is also enjoying a revival among top secretaries, and many employers are prepared to pay a high price to get it. The secretary who is able to assume the role of manager and IP specialist is guaranteed a high salary and prestigious position in the organization.

- **Specialisms**: it's thought that some specialist secretarial training (e.g. medical, agricultural, language skills) will be taught as optional modules within NVQs. There's some concern that this may in some way dilute the levels of competence and professionalism of specialist secretaries; but experts will always be needed, and the possession of NVQs at level 3 or above may help to enhance salary levels. Because of the modular structure of the new national qualifications, we may also see new types of specialist emerge in the form of secretaries who have chosen to take certain modules (e.g. text production) to a very high level.

- **Career progression**: most professional organizations believe that the new system of vocational qualifications will help to structure the profession and create a system of career grading and progression which has never existed before.

A career in crisis?

Falling school rolls have alerted employers all over Britain to a disturbing trend: the number of sixteen-to twenty-four-year-olds is declining dramatically and is set to do so for some years to come. Employers in every field of work are in direct competition with each other for the dwindling reserves of labour, which leads to the inevitable question: can secretarial work compete?

Children are taught to be successful and competitive, and as the economic situation has improved over the last few years school leavers have begun to expect more from their careers. Secretarial work (at least in the South East) pays well, offers relative security of tenure and doesn't carry as much stress as junior management jobs which may pay less.

On the other hand, the secretary – however well regarded and however well paid – will always be 'number two'. Up to now taking a secretarial course has frequently been seen as a good move because it teaches useful skills and may help a young person to get into a chosen area of work 'by the back door'. The advent of National Vocational Qualifications will make it much harder to become a qualified secretary, because it will take several years to acquire the necessary study units and work experience. Since other professions will also be graded on the same national scale, it should be just as easy to study to be, say, an accountant or an engineer – professions which rightly or wrongly both still carry more kudos than that of the secretary.

Secretarial work is going to have to make itself very attractive indeed if it's going to find sufficient recruits over the next few years. Nor will it be enough to concentrate on sixteen-to twenty-four-year-old girls: the profession also has to attract older women and men of all ages. In an interview in *Weekend* (3 December 1988), Michael Yorke of Reed Employment said: 'Employers are going to have to change if they want a reasonable flow of candidates for jobs. Market pressures are going to bring about a change and it's already starting to happen.' If employers don't abandon their prejudices, the price of skilled secretarial labour seems set to rise to even more unlikely levels.

Older women are certainly queuing up to get back into secretarial work, particularly if hours and conditions can be tailored to fit their domestic circumstances. But will men be so quick to respond to the call? Margaret Evans of the London Chamber of Commerce and Industry feels that 'there is no reason why they shouldn't come back into secretarial work . . . but I think it will take a long time, because it has become so stereotyped.'

Although Miss Evans is not optimistic about the prospects of a massive influx of male recruits, she's very much aware of the special role which male secretaries can fulfil:

I have heard a lot of people say that they have considerable difficulties in business meetings involving the Middle East if they have a female secretary. They have to get a man from somewhere – one who is reasonably good at English and can take notes – who then has to go out and regurgitate it all to somebody else who types it up. If they had a male secretary he could do the whole job. Some people would also argue that male secretaries are useful in the so-called 'heavy' industries.

Desperate remedies

Secretarial work is very much a seller's market at the moment. The top secretary can virtually name his or her price and desperate employers will pay it.

However, as survey results indicate, money is not the prime motivator for secretarial workers. If they are not to desert the profession in search of something 'better', the job must be made more attractive and individuals given the space in which to develop their potential.

In the article 'Putting secretaries in their place', Dr Susan Vinnicombe and Dr Nina Colwill point out that attitudes must change if secretaries' jobs are to be enhanced, rather than damaged, by new technology. They suggest that all organizations employing secretaries should implement a strategy based on the following 'key' areas:

- *Job descriptions*: jobs should be properly analysed and a grading structure established according to job content rather than on the boss's status;
- *Recruitment*: people should be carefully matched to jobs, instead of chosen because they match 'the boss's vision of his ideal secretary';
- *Salary*: secretarial salaries should be linked to the value of the job, not to the status of the boss;
- *Performance appraisal*: salary increases should be based on merit. Performance objectives should be set systematically; this will help managers recognize the value of their secretaries;
- *Team building*: managers should work closely with their secretaries and involve them in all aspects of the boss's job (including visits, talks and group meetings);
- *Career development*: managers should involve themselves in counselling their secretaries on their work and career development; secretarial work is 'an ideal training ground for management';

- *Training and personal development*: secretaries should not be overlooked in the management training and development area; even if secretaries do not want to move up in their careers, they should have the chance to keep abreast of new management ideas and techniques.

All this sounds extremely sensible and positive. Unfortunately, the findings of the 1987 Industrial Society survey were that 'only 24% of secretaries attend personal development courses. 42% consider they have little chance of promotion.'

A secretary for tomorrow

Tomorrow's secretary will demand the professional status and career structure which other professionals accept as automatic. The new system of National Vocational Qualifications will have to prove itself; but if it works secretaries can expect to acquire, for the first time, a status which is not based on that of their bosses.

According to Margaret Evans, herself involved in NCVQ:

The secretary – whatever title is used in the future – is going to be much more of an Executive Assistant. This is not just a person who does what he or she is told by the manager; it's a person who is involved enough to suggest a solution to problems when they arise. The person likely to succeed in the future is still likely to be the person with years of experience in traditional secretarial skills, and who is very, very comfortable and at home with technology.

Male or female, young or middle-aged, the secretary of tomorrow will occupy an important place in the economic life of this country – but will anyone want to be 'number two' any more? And even if people are willing to become secretaries, can the astounding boom in jobs and salaries be expected to continue? Even in periods of economic recession secretaries are needed, but only the very best survive.

The next five years should see quite a considerable change in the world of secretarial work – and we will certainly be awaiting further developments with interest.

The secretary

Hers is the one smiling face left
In a humourless world:
Profit and loss, and the exigencies
Of time and money,
Somehow are tempered in this admirable image
Of great calm.

Hers is the confidence, the competence
Of those who know their power is absolute.
She lifts her finger – godlike – and from chaos
Order reigns. Priestess of all the mysteries,
The oracle: the undisputed queen.

Knowledge, experience and skills
Are all the armoury she needs
To win herself a kingdom.
She may feel fear,
But never shows it: works to display
Complete control.

Others rely on her to get things done:
But she relies on no-one
Save herself: accepting blame,
She never claims more credit
Than her due.

Corporate slave or superwoman:
White witch; or just vice-captain of the team?
The underling who grew to be your equal –
Now:
Do you dare to dream without her?

Sue Dyson

Useful Addresses

Institute of Agricultural Secretaries (IAS)
NAC
Stoneleigh
KENILWORTH
Warwickshire CV8 2LZ (Tel 0203–696592)

Association of Legal Secretaries (ALS)
The Mill
Clymping
Nr LITTLEHAMPTON
West Sussex BN17 5NR

Association of Medical Secretaries, Practice Administrators and
Receptionists (AMSPAR)
Tavistock House North
Tavistock Square
LONDON WC1H 9LN (Tel 01–387 6005)

Institute of Qualified Private Secretaries Ltd (IQPS)
Assistant Secretary
126 Farnham Road
SLOUGH
Berks SL1 4XA

European Association of Professional Secretaries (EAPS)
c/o Wendy Syer
Abbey National Building Society
Abbey House
Baker Street
LONDON NW1 6XL

Association of Personal Assistants and Secretaries Ltd (APAS)
14 Victoria Terrace
ROYAL LEAMINGTON SPA
Warwickshire

National Council for Vocational Qualifications (NCVQ)
222 Euston Road
LONDON NW1 2BZ (Tel 01–387 9898)

TUC Organisation and Industrial Relations Department
Congress House
Great Russell Street
LONDON WC1B 3LS (Tel 01–636 4030)

General, Municipal, Boilermakers and Allied Trades Union (GMU)
Thorne House
Ruxley Ridge
Claygate
ESHER
Surrey KT10 0TL

Association of Professional, Executive, Clerical and Computer Staff (APEX)
22 Worple Road
LONDON SW19 4DF

London Chamber of Commerce and Industry Examinations Board
Marlowe House
Station Road
SIDCUP
Kent (Tel 01–302 0261)

Royal Society of Arts Examinations Board
Murray Road
ORPINGTON
Kent (Tel 0689–32421)

Women in Management
64 Marryat Road
Wimbledon
LONDON SW19 (Tel 01–946 1238)

The Industrial Society
3 Carlton House Terrace
LONDON SW1

Equal Opportunities Commission
1 Bedford Street
LONDON WC2 (Tel 01–379 6323)

Index